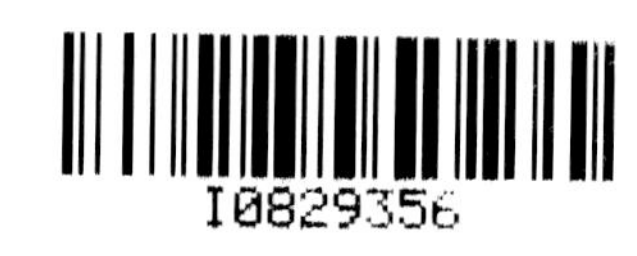

This Coloring Book

Belongs To:

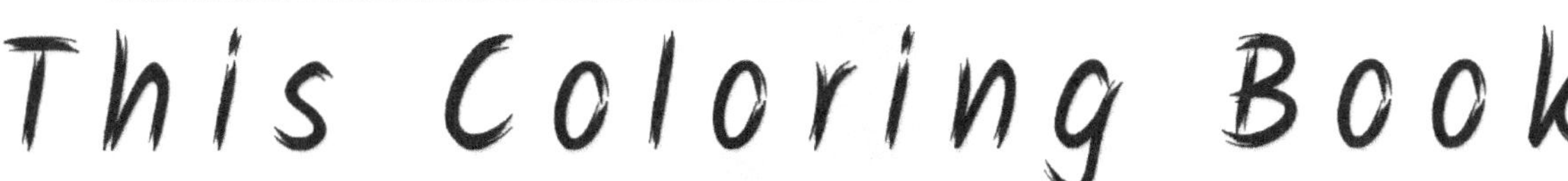

HAPPY NEW **YEAR**

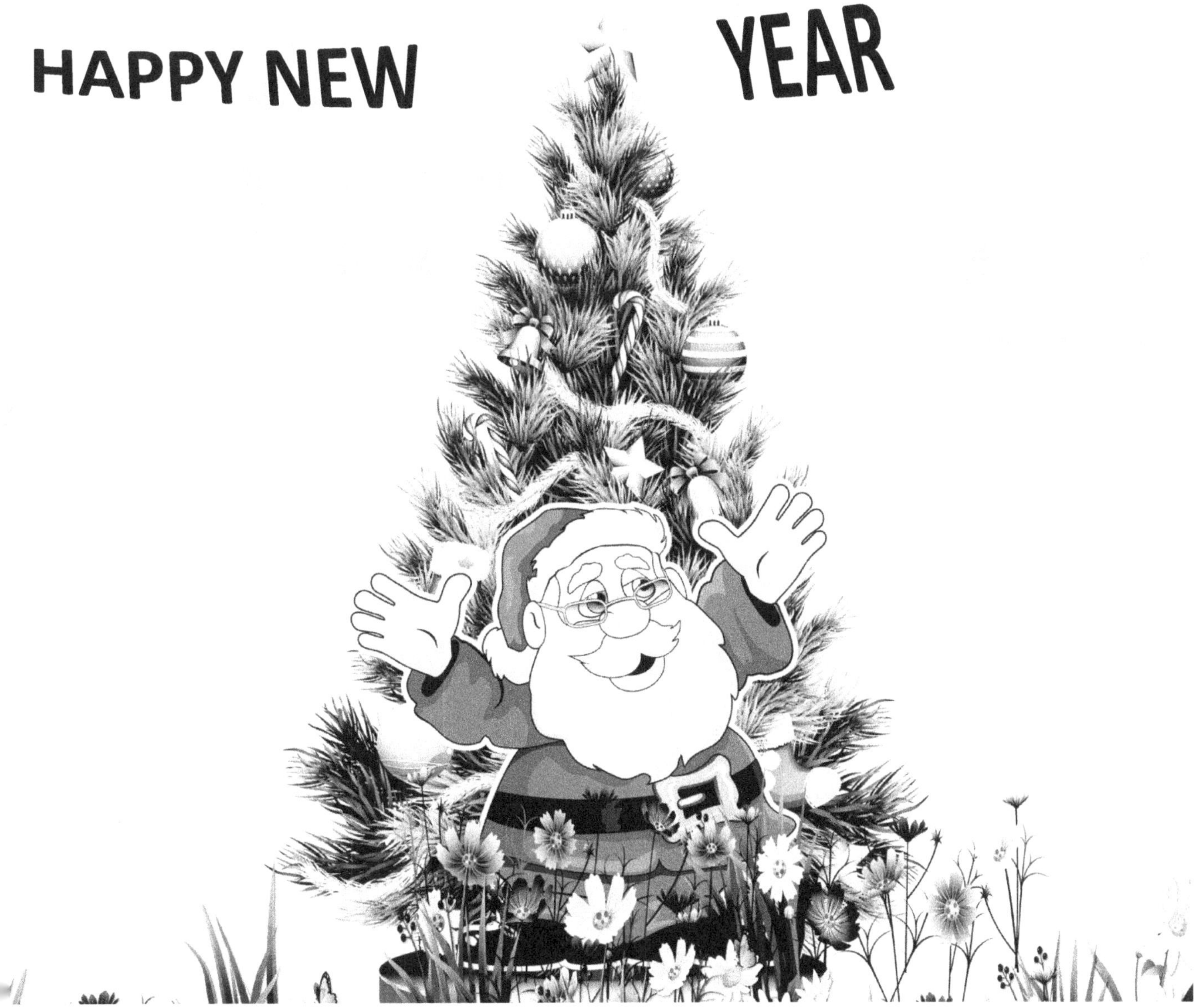

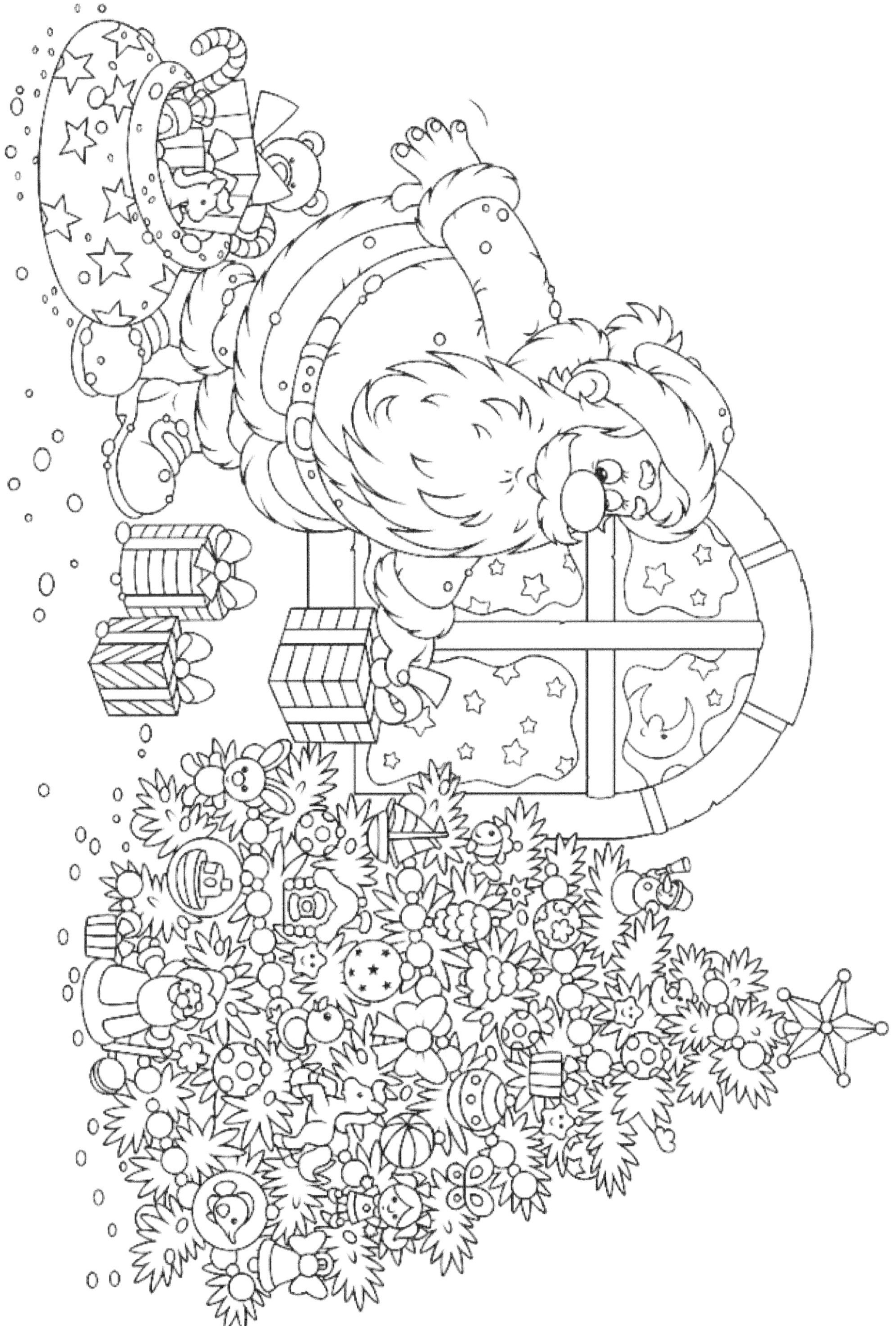

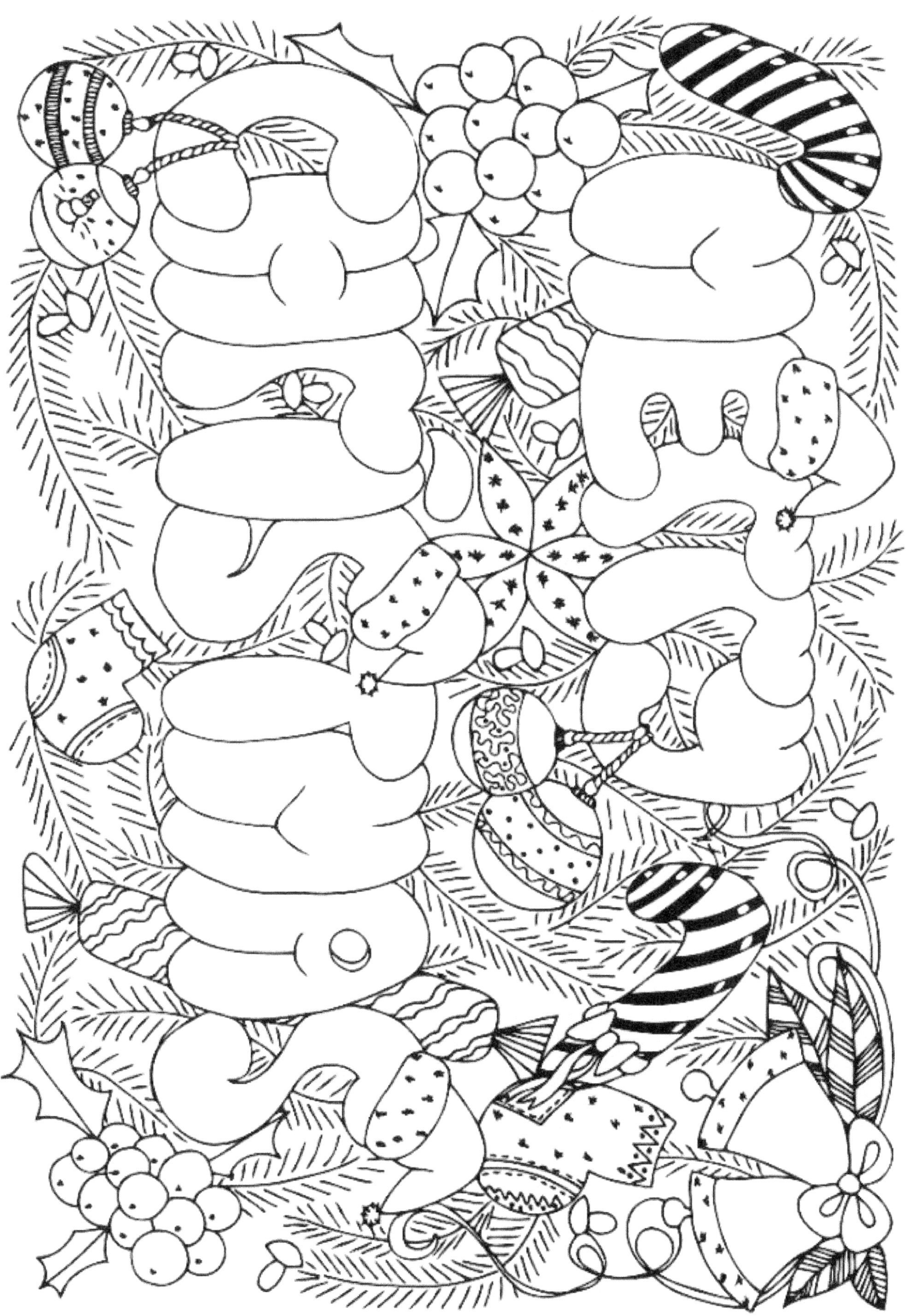

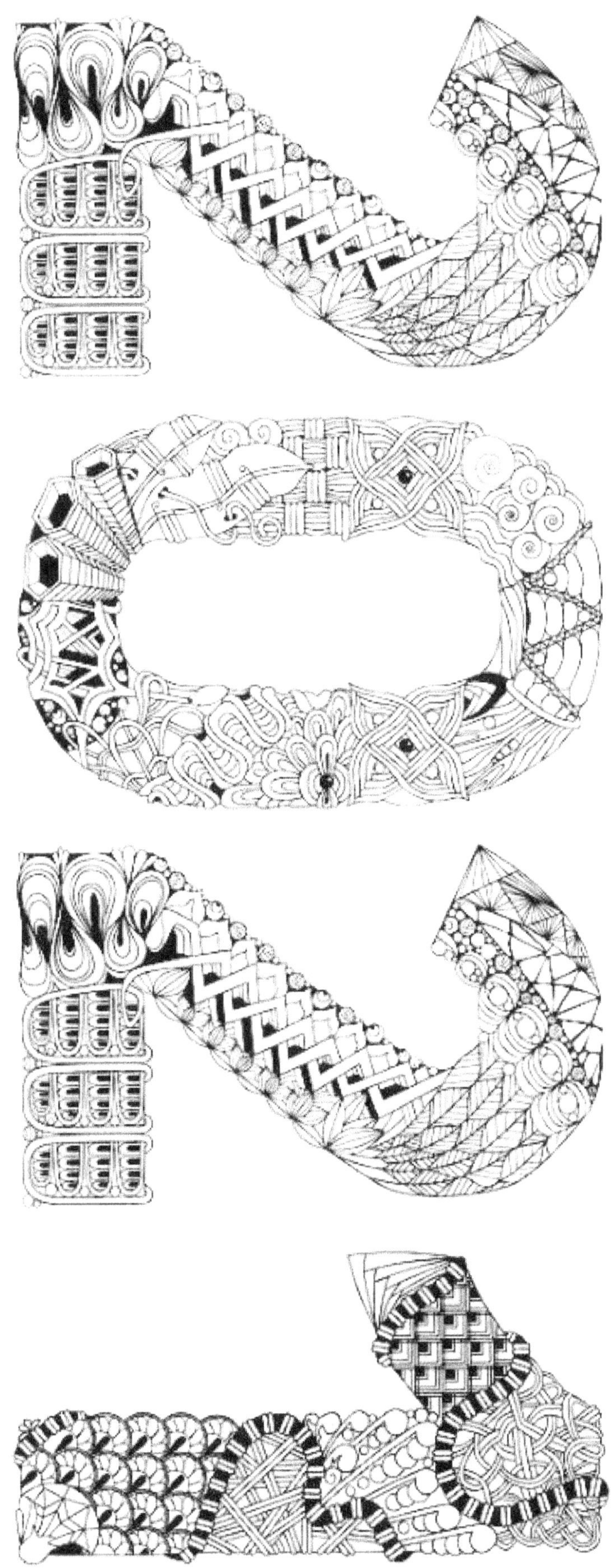

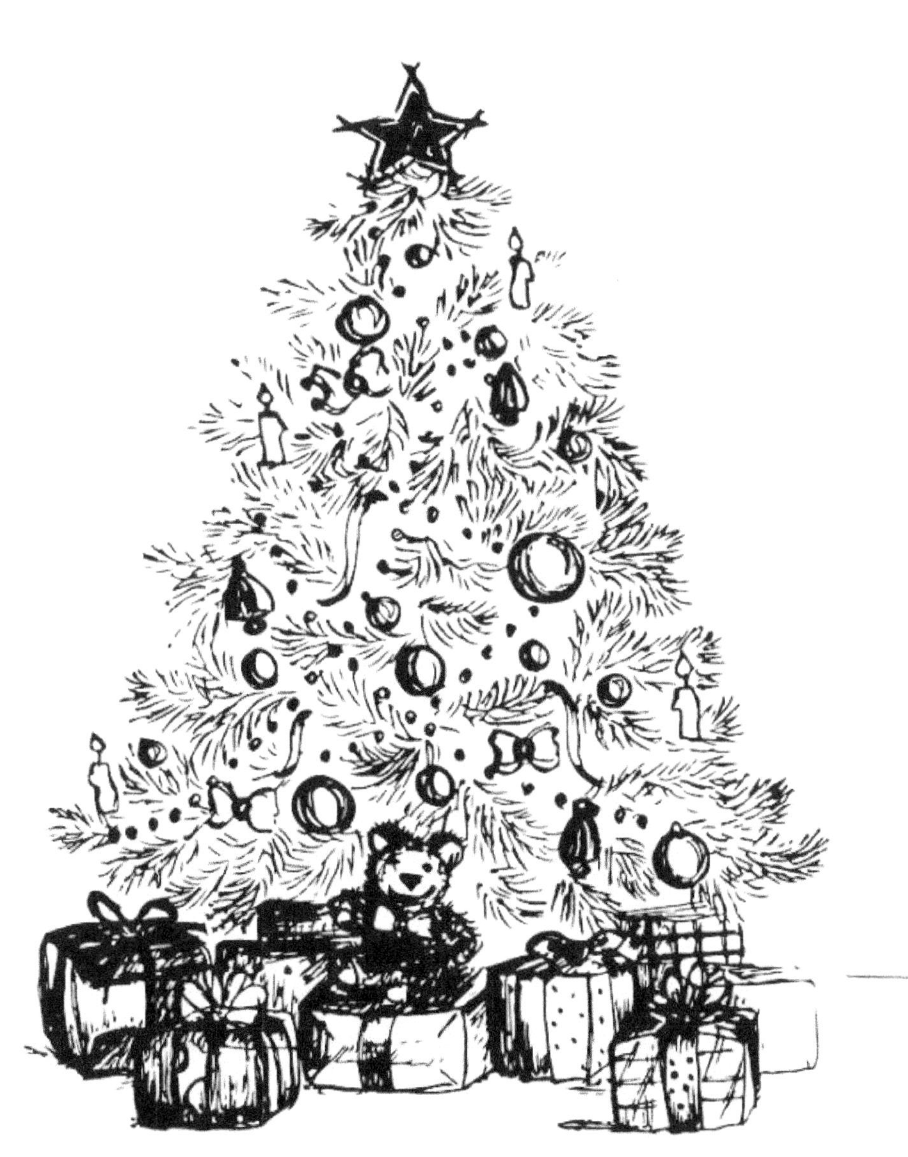

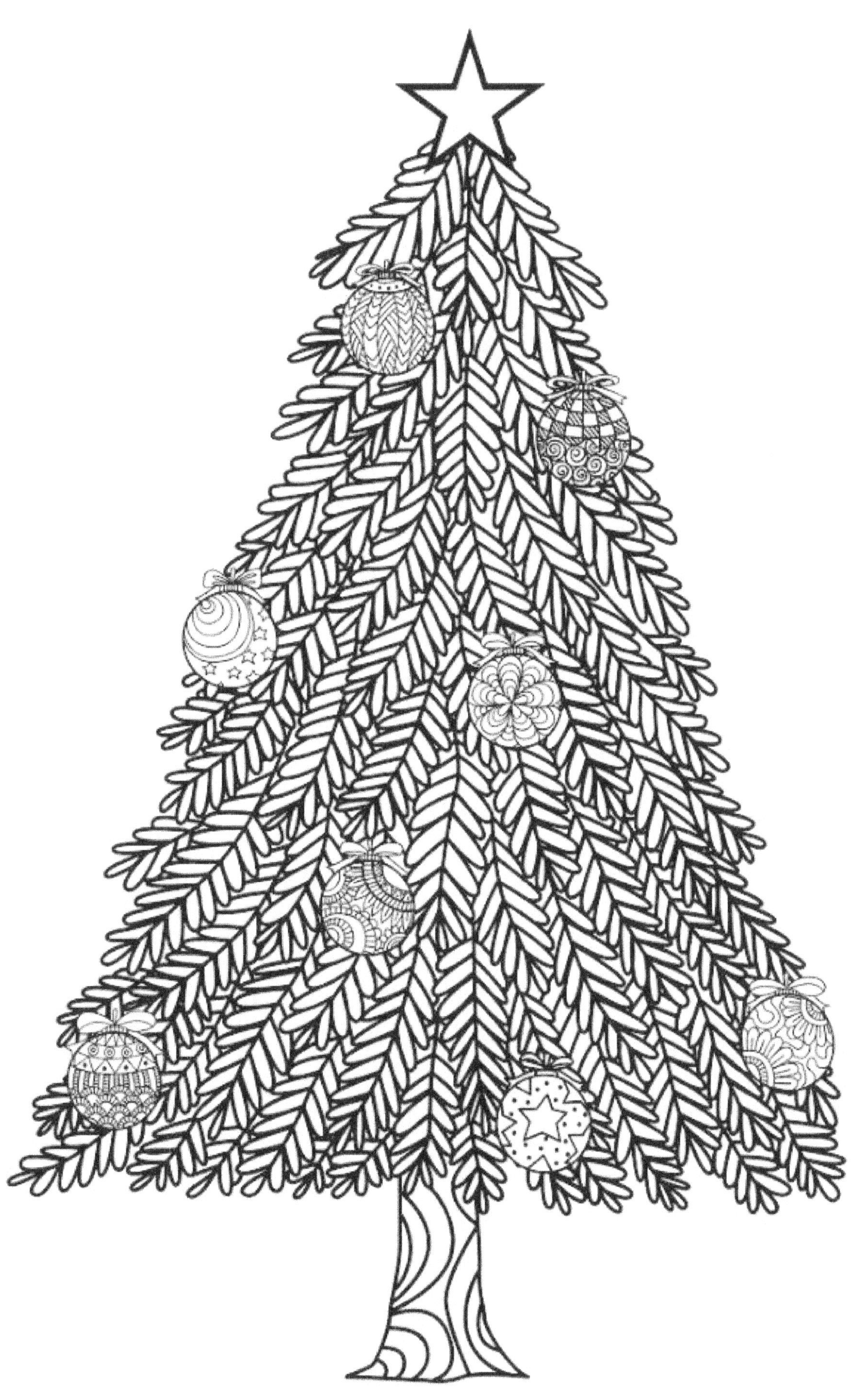

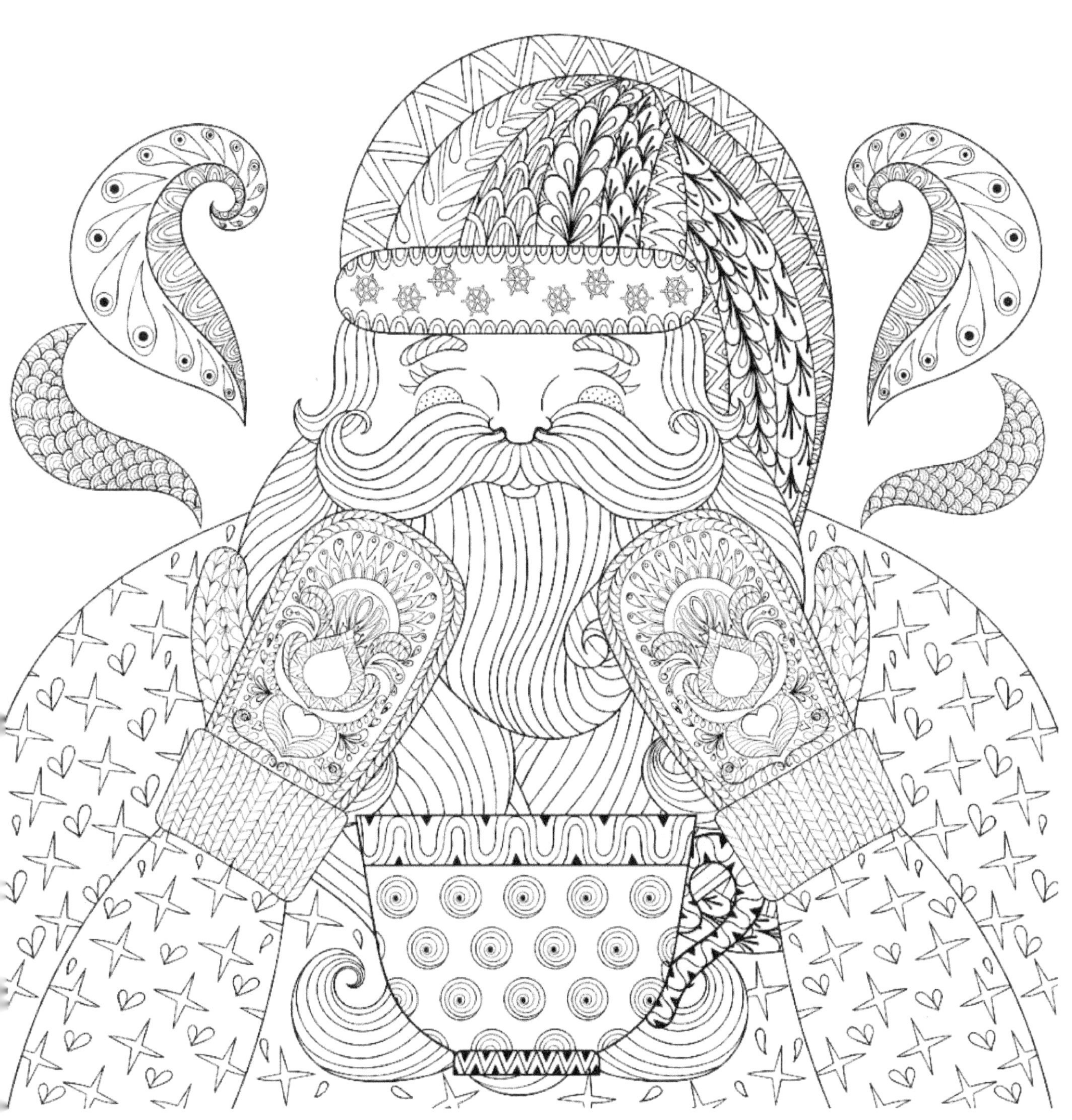

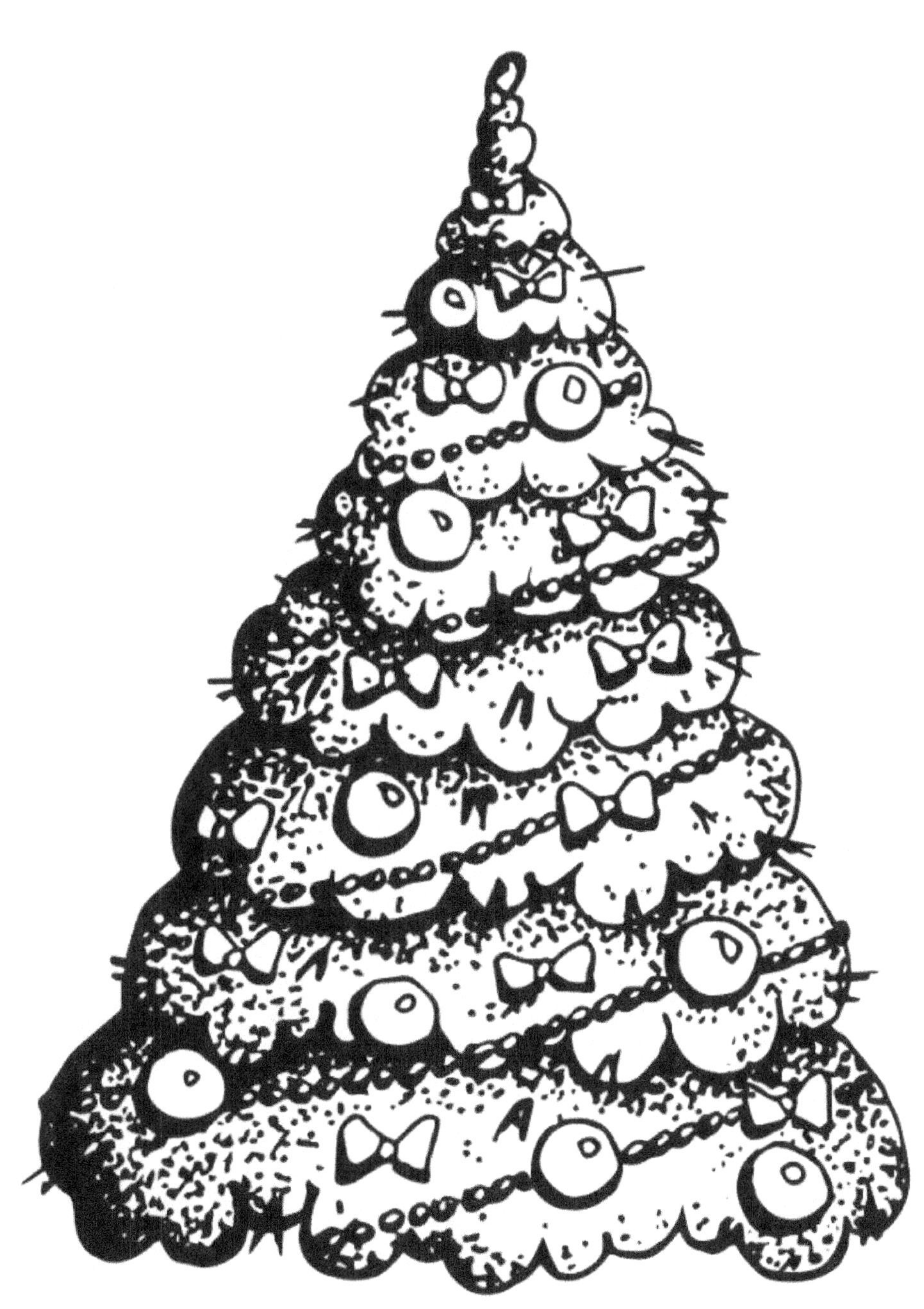

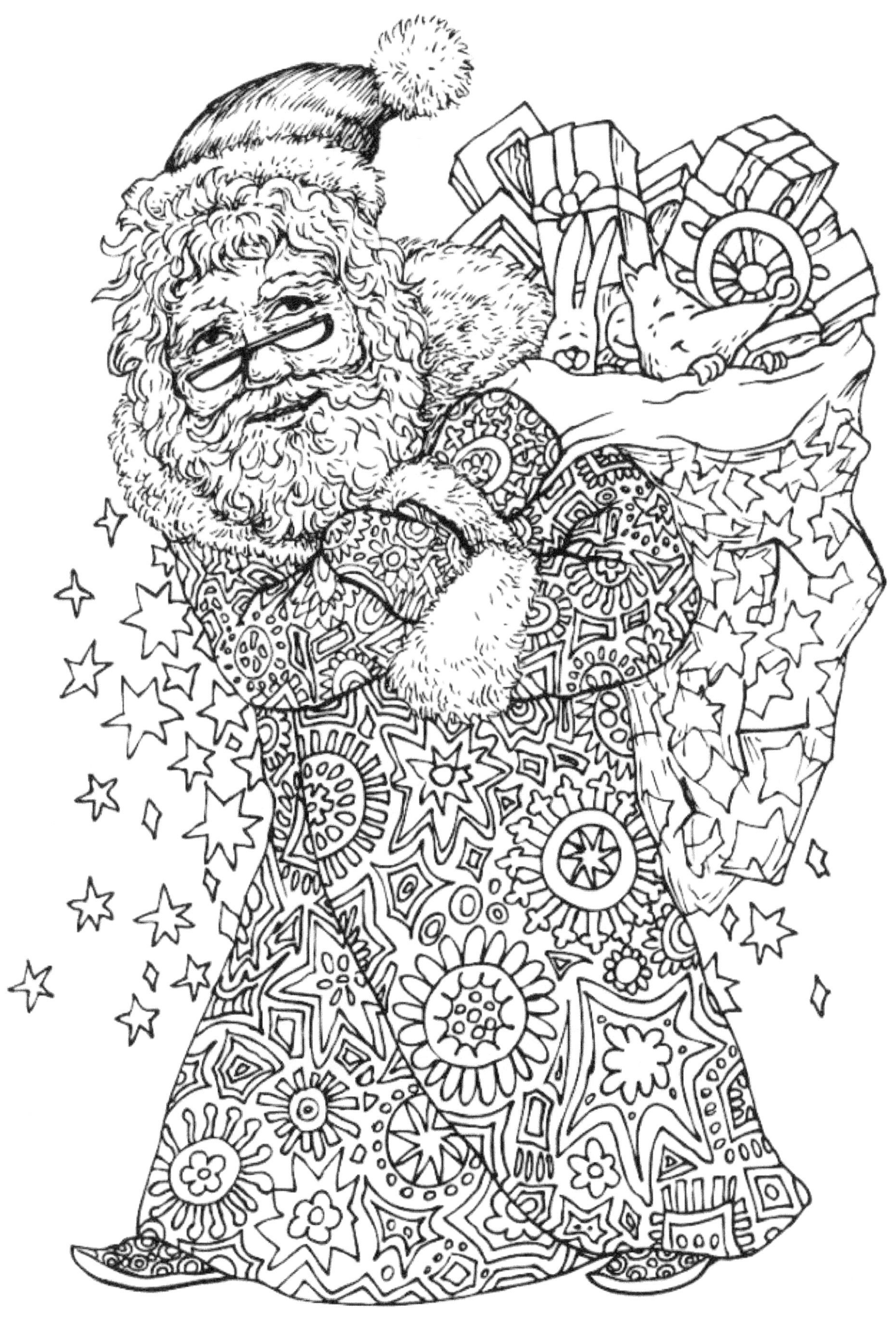

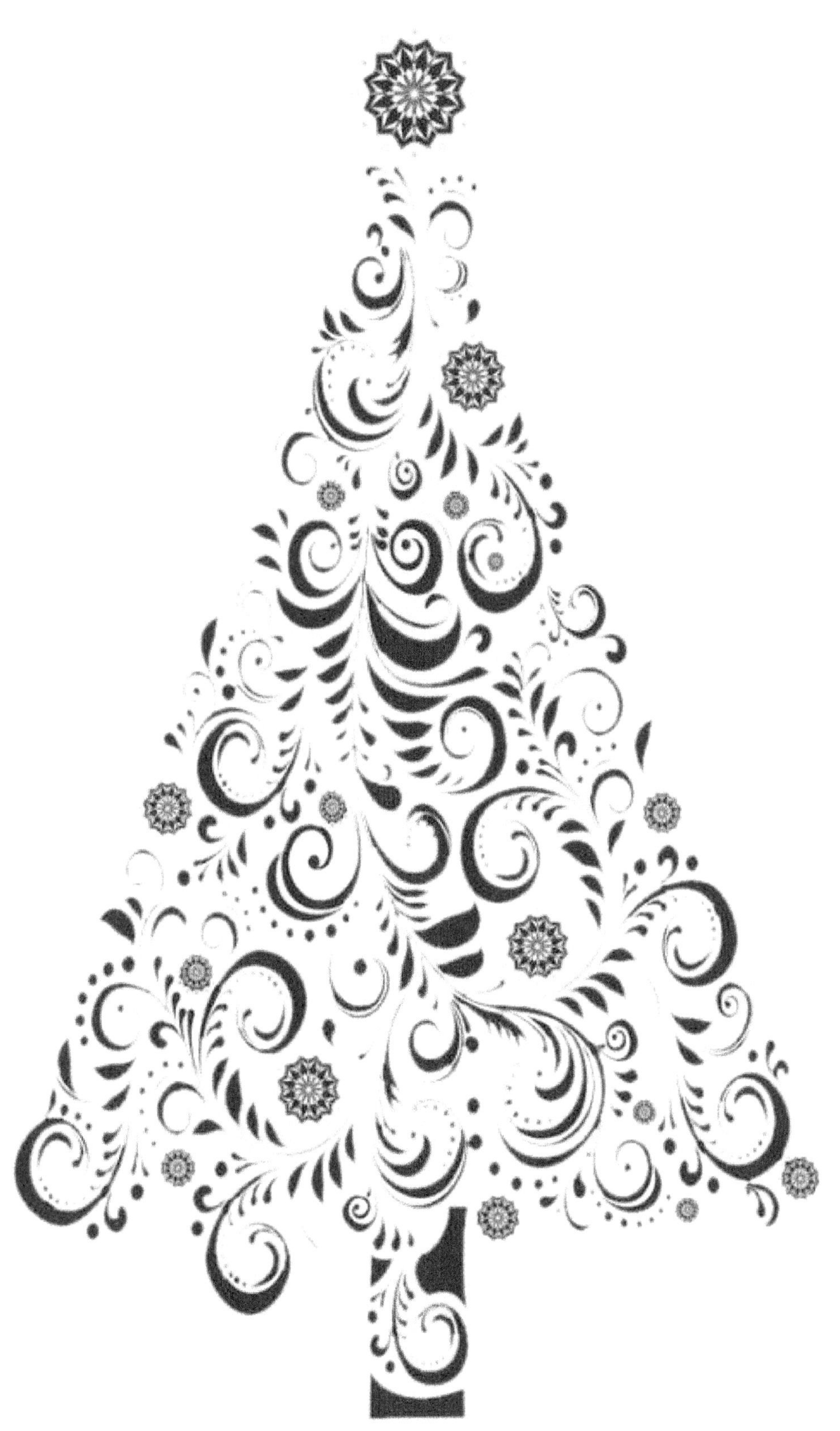

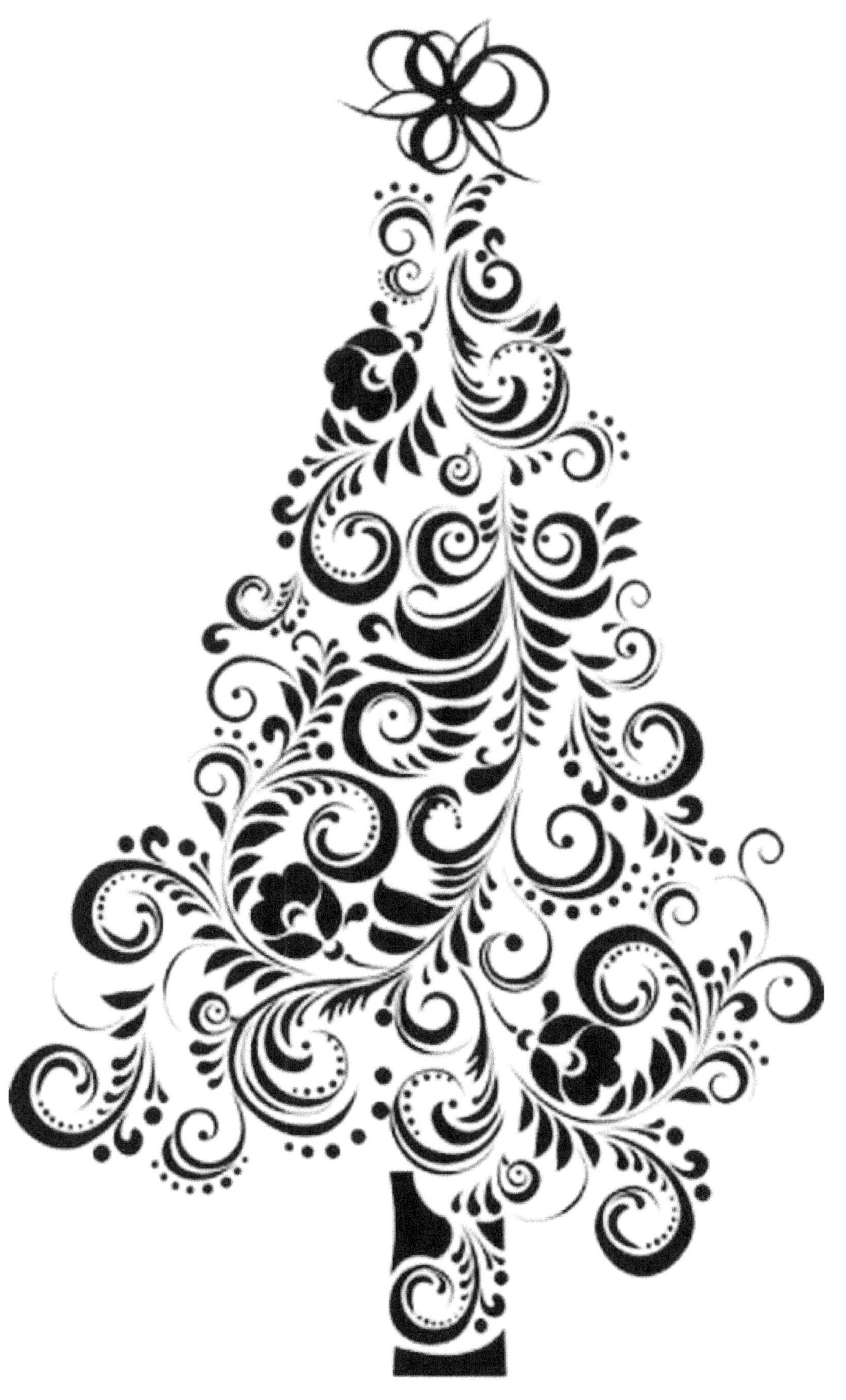

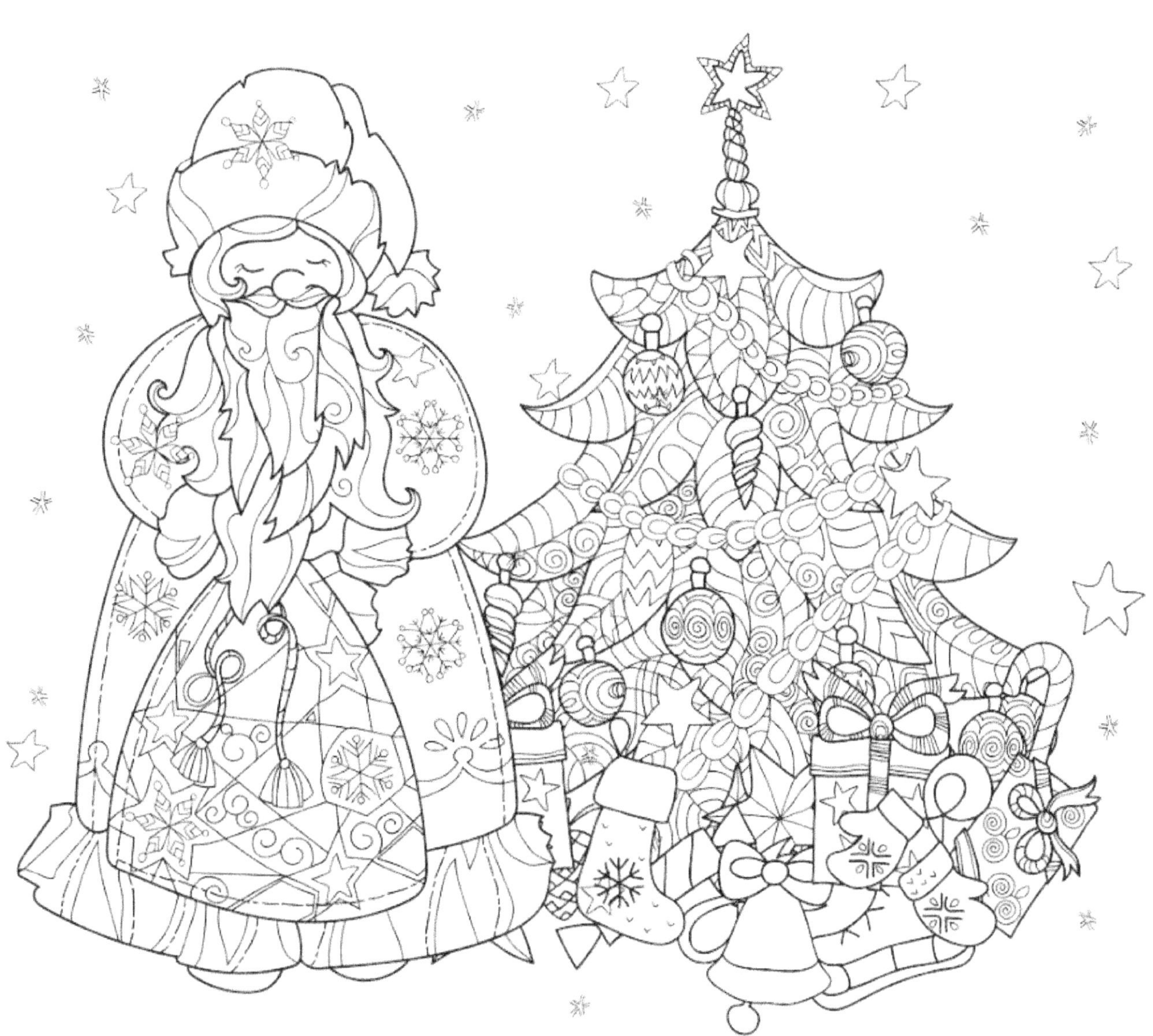

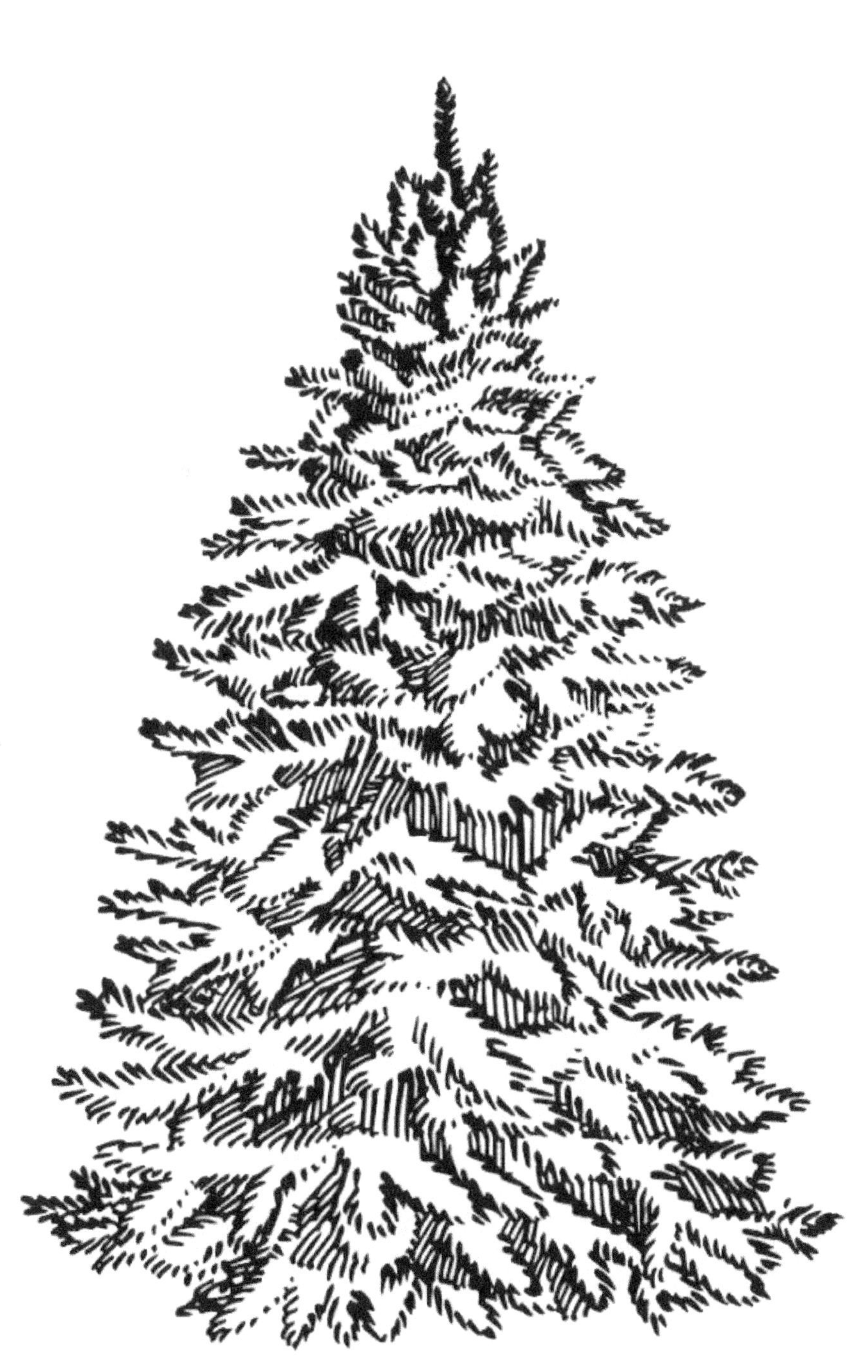

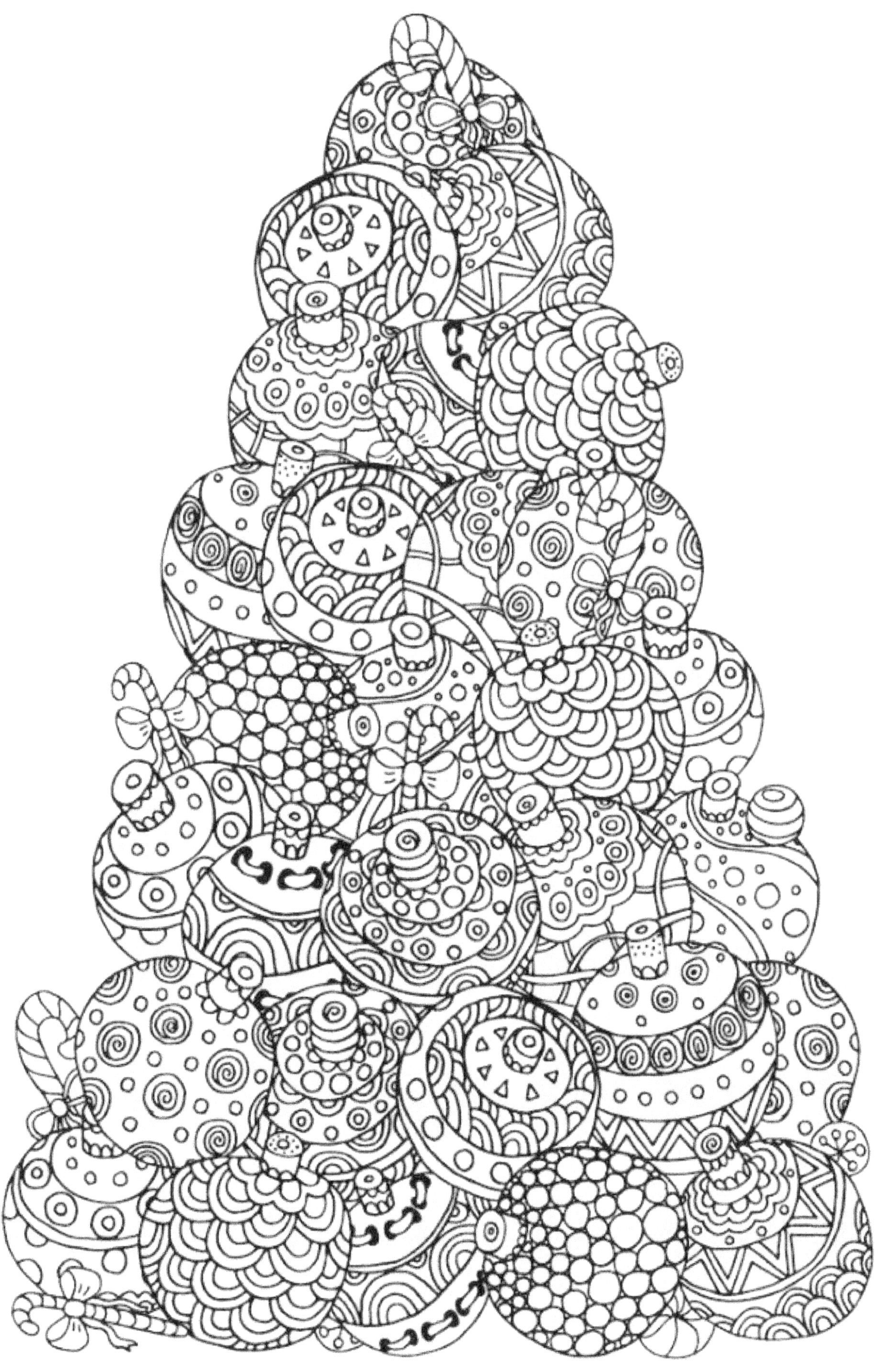

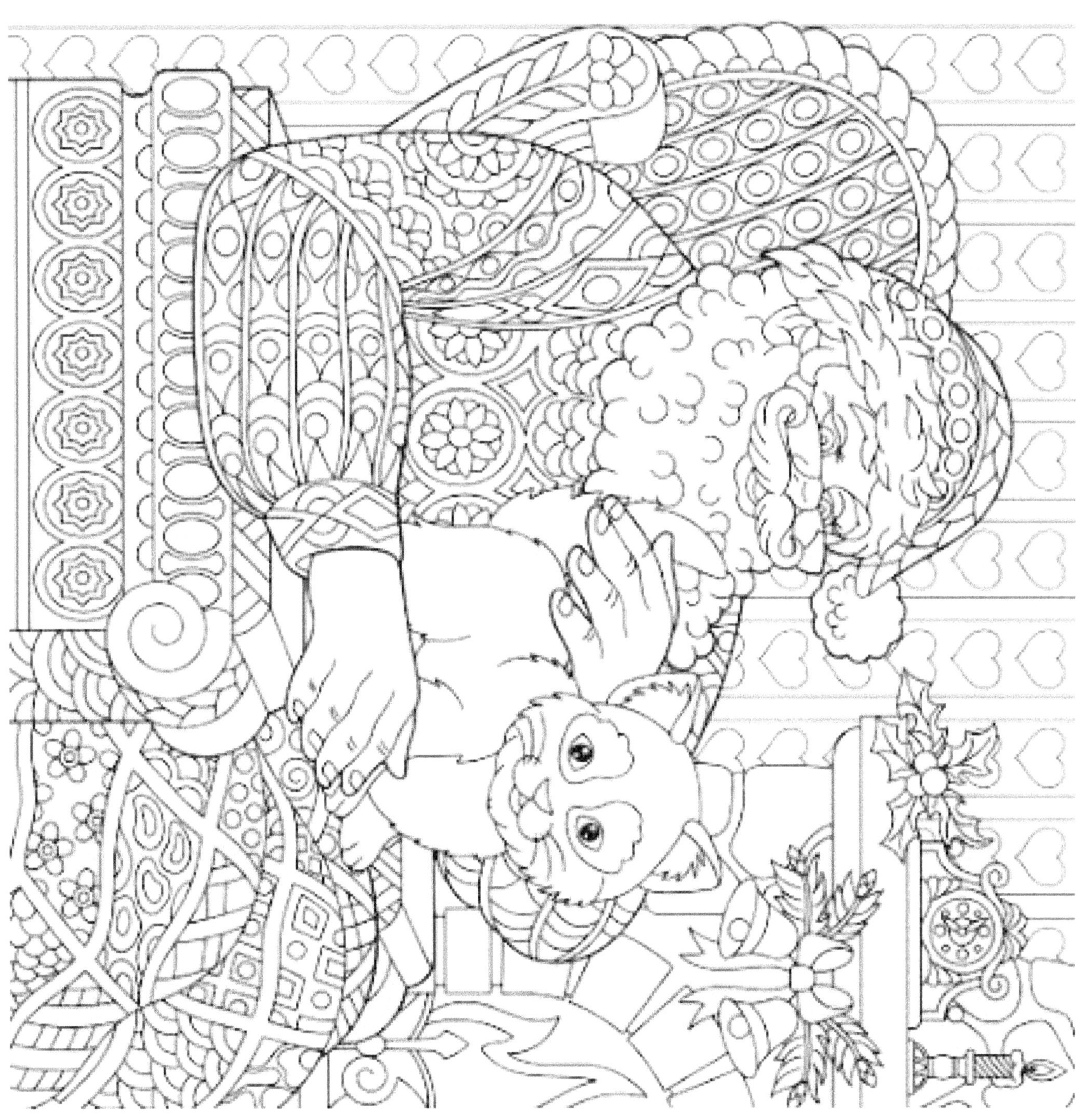

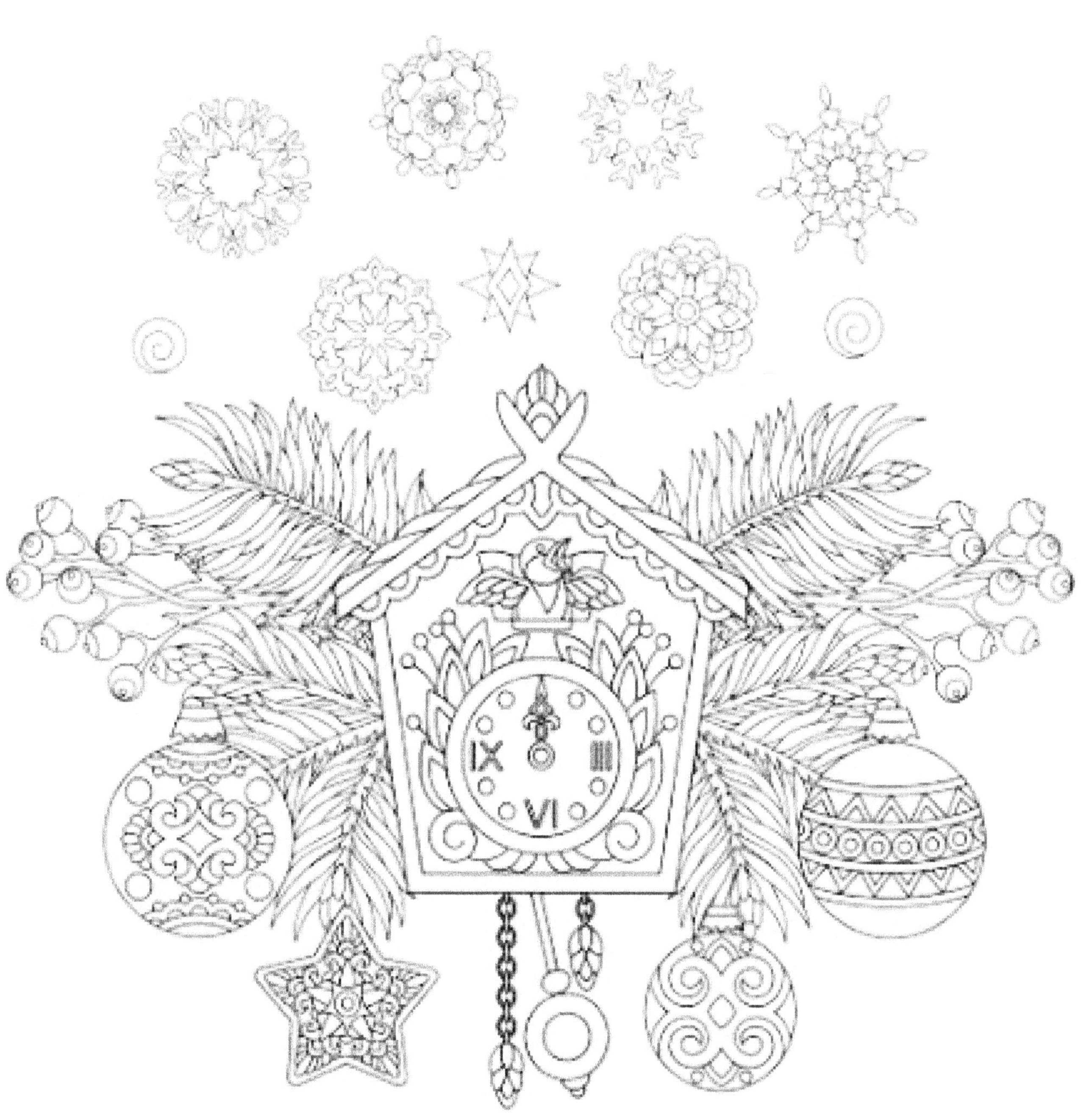

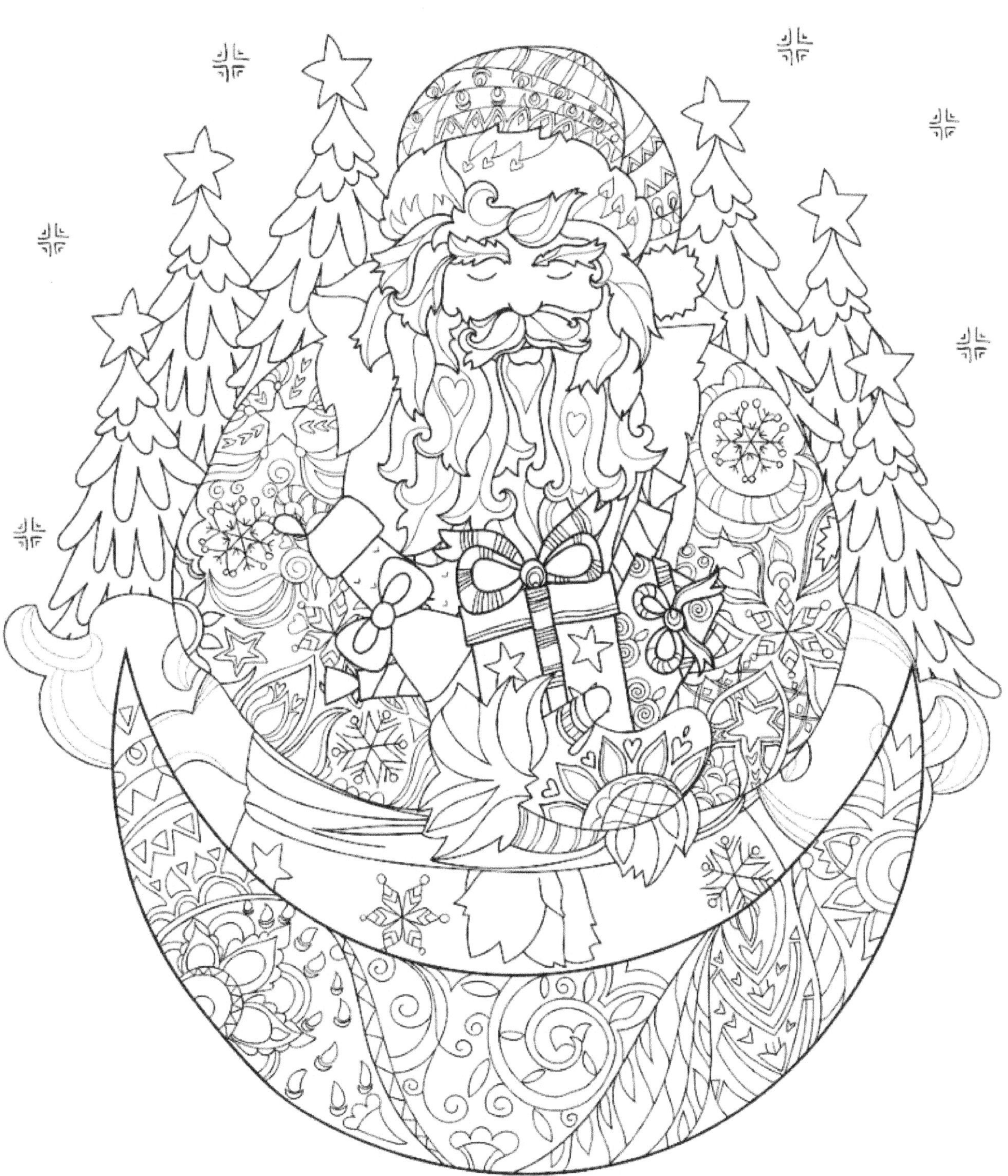

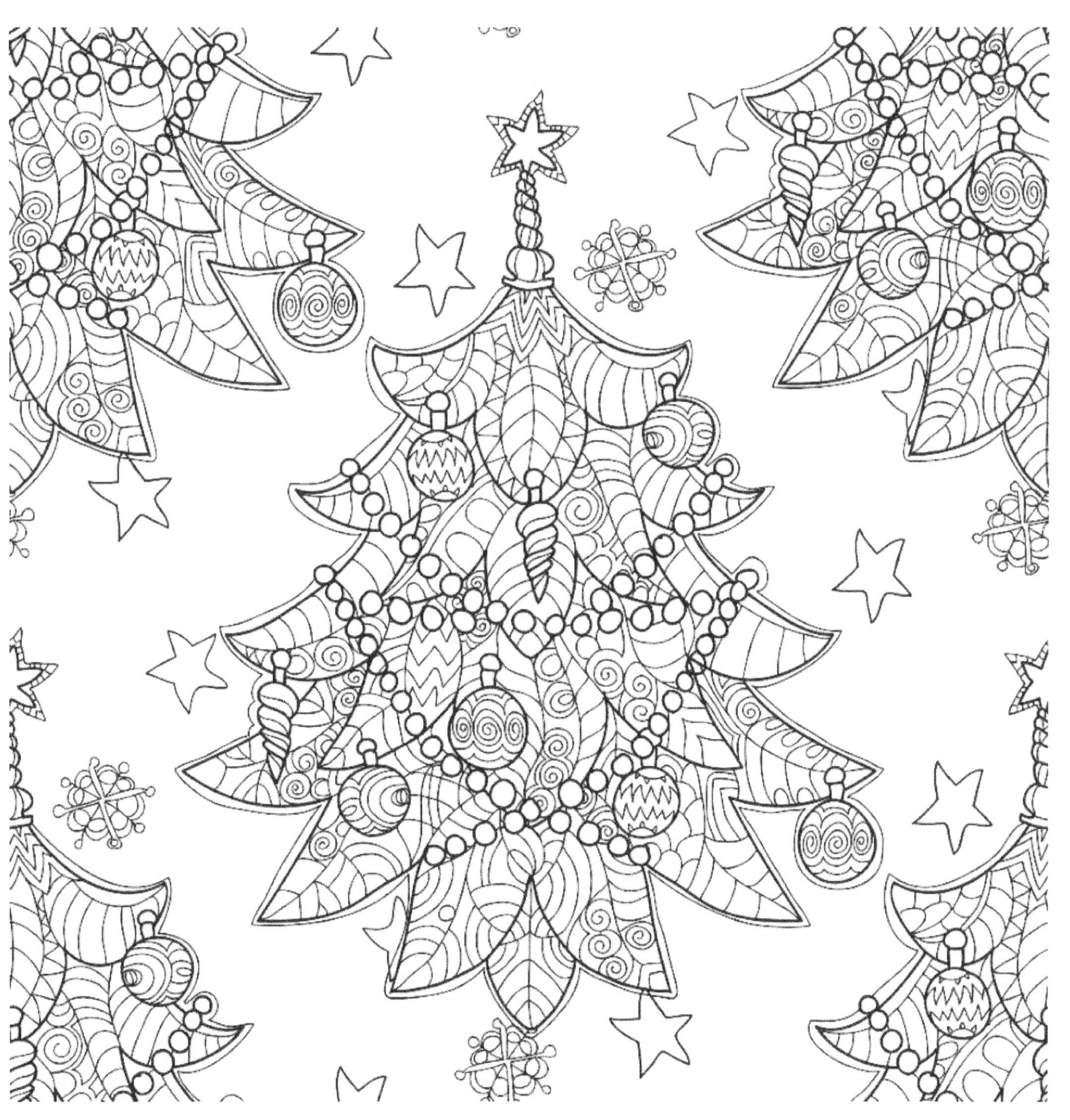

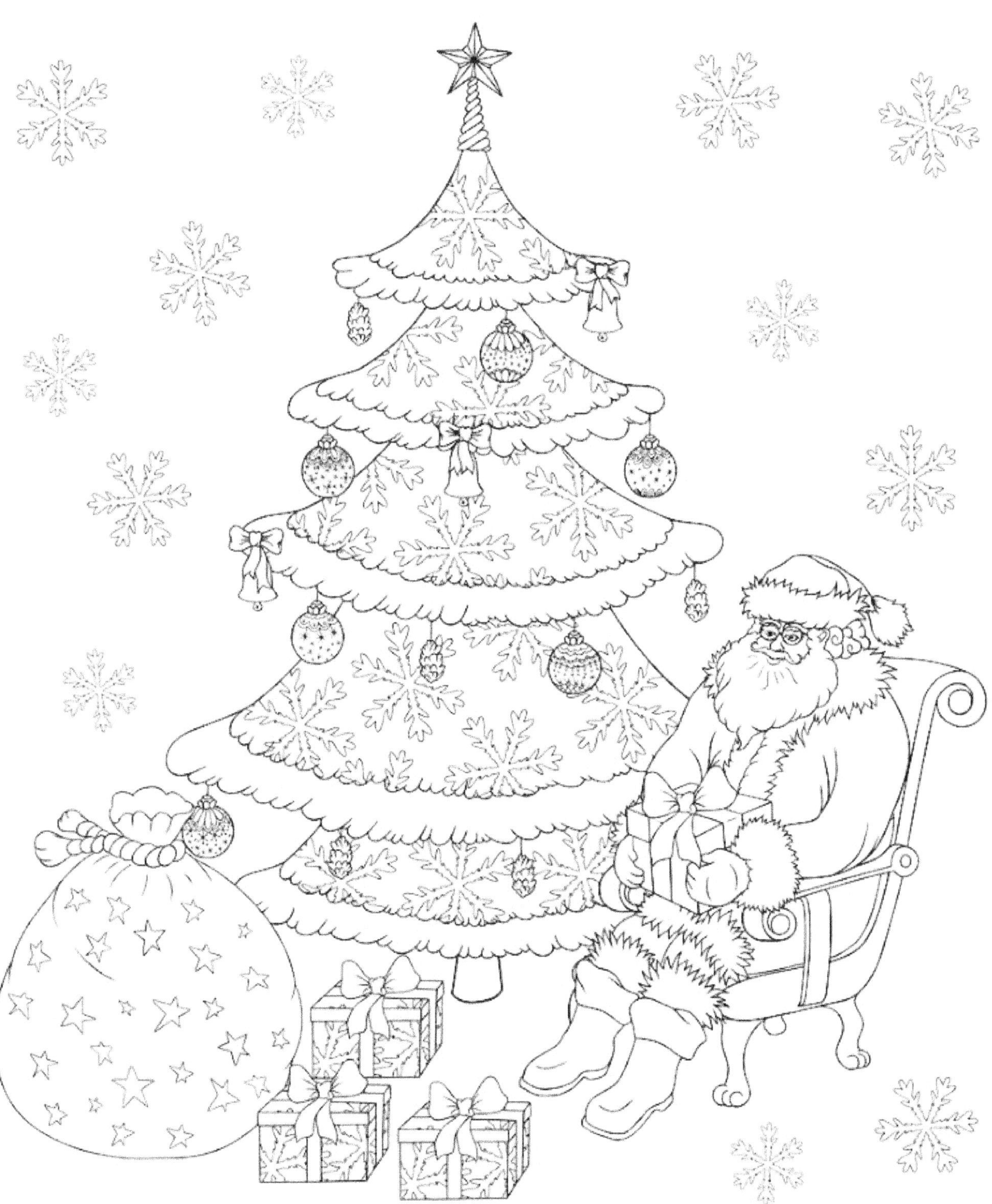

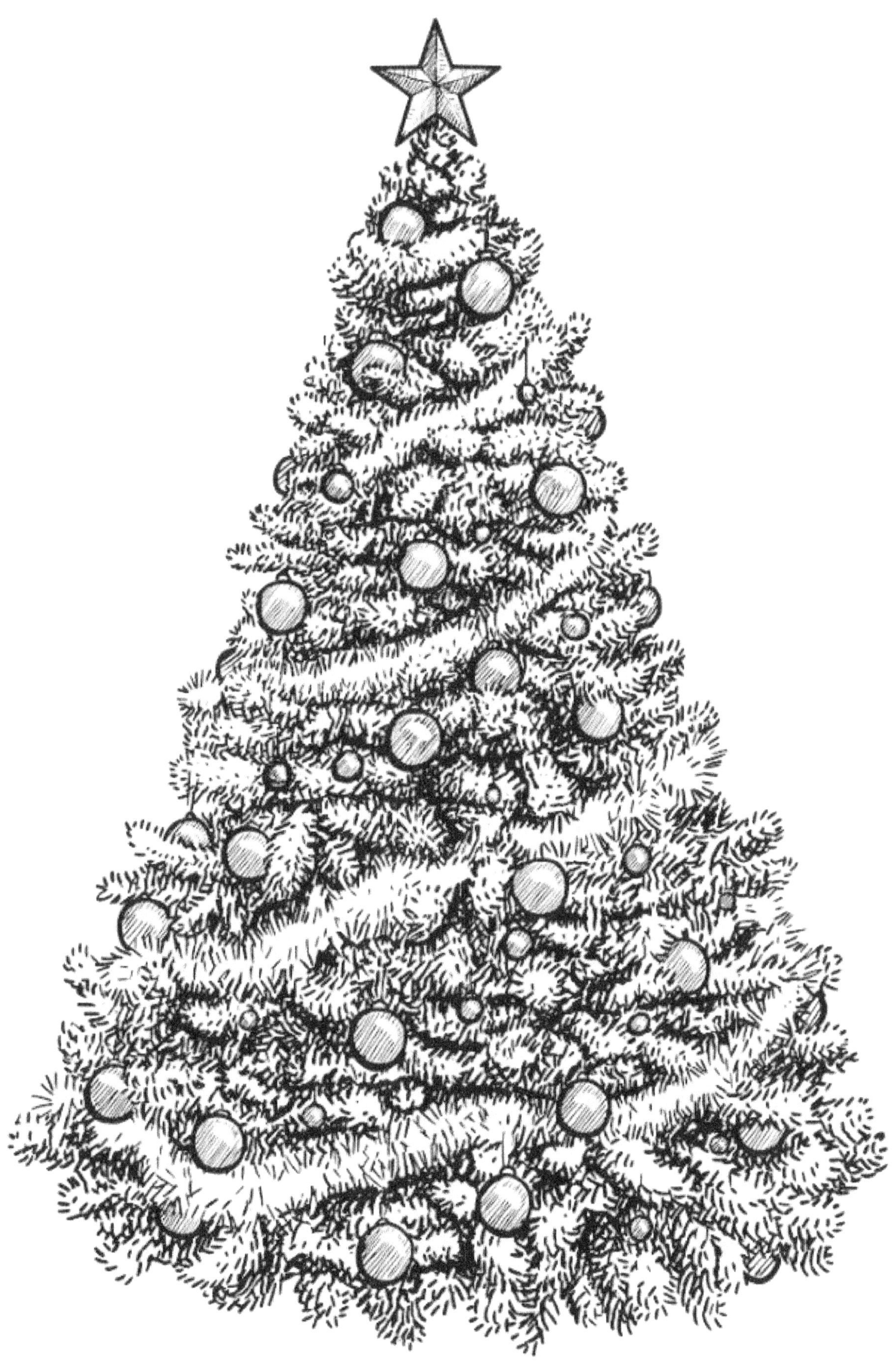

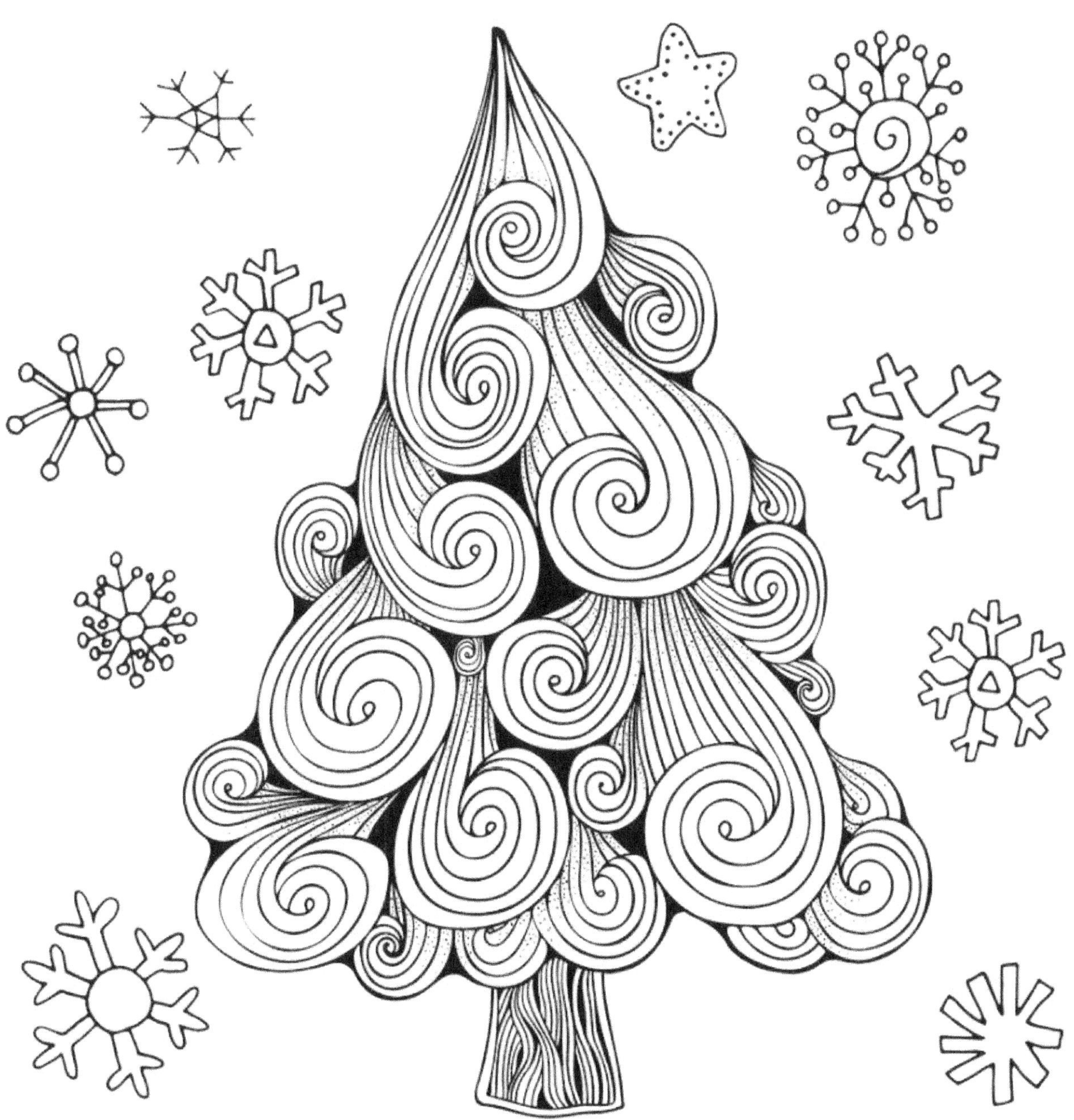

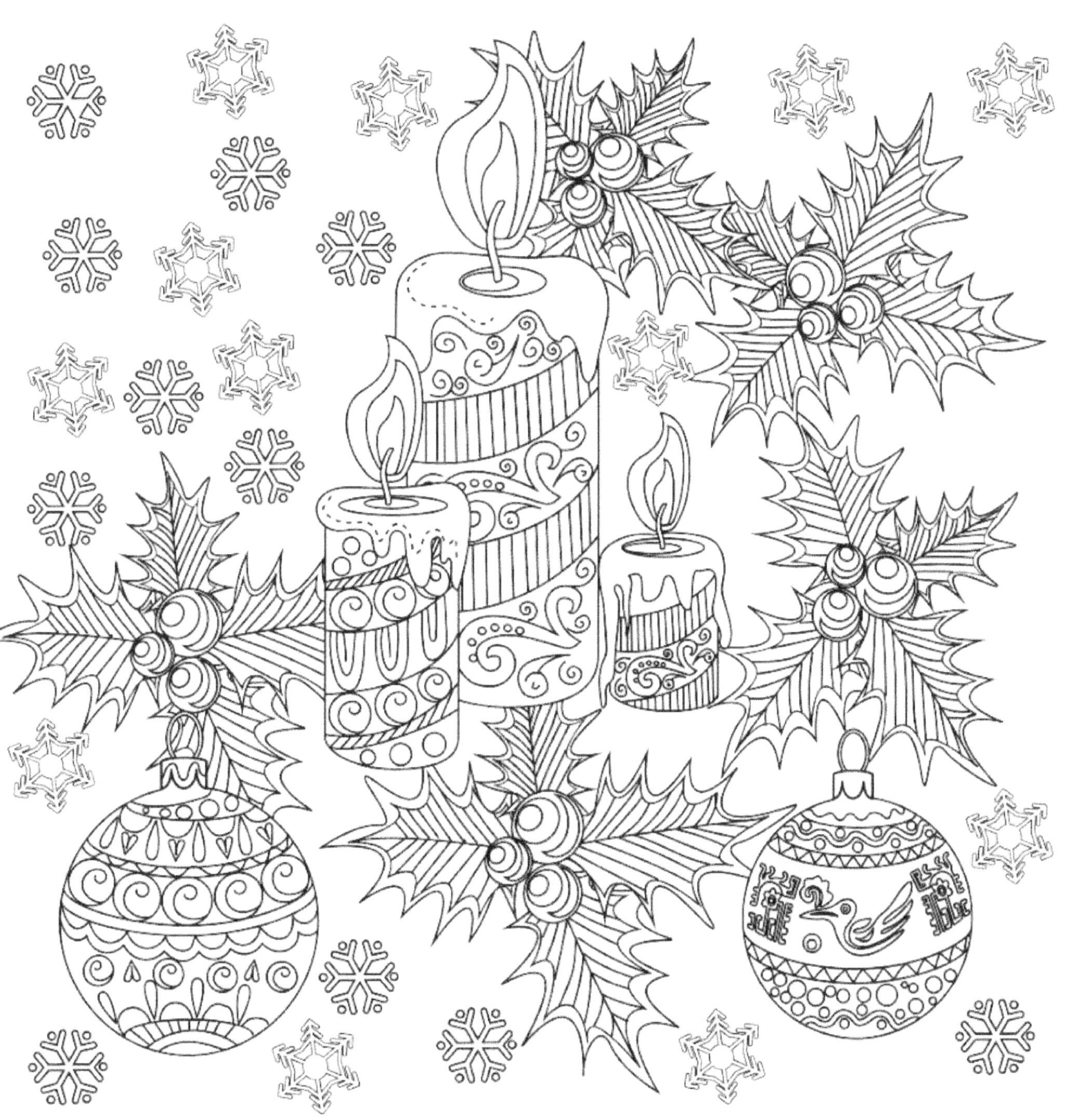

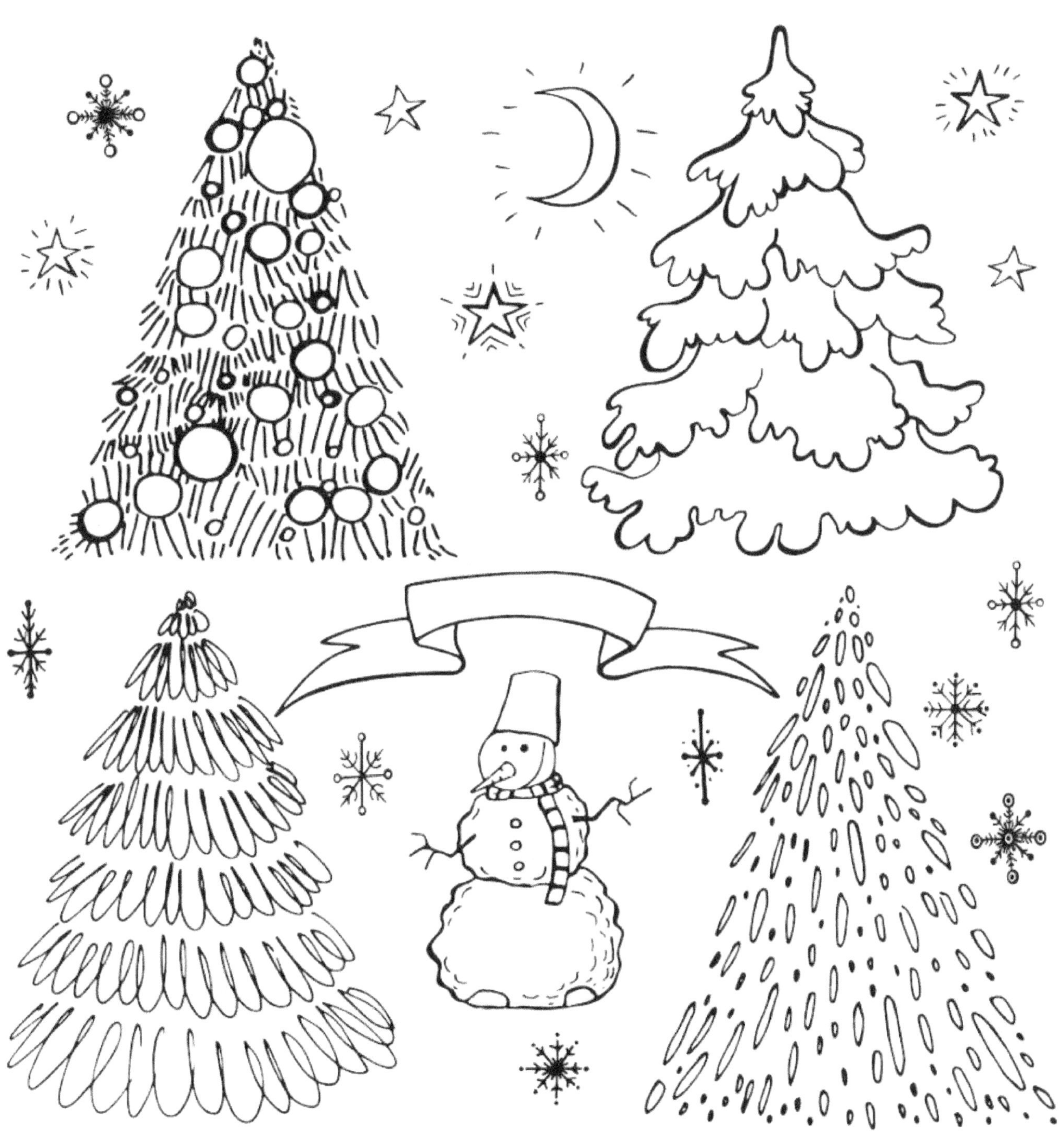

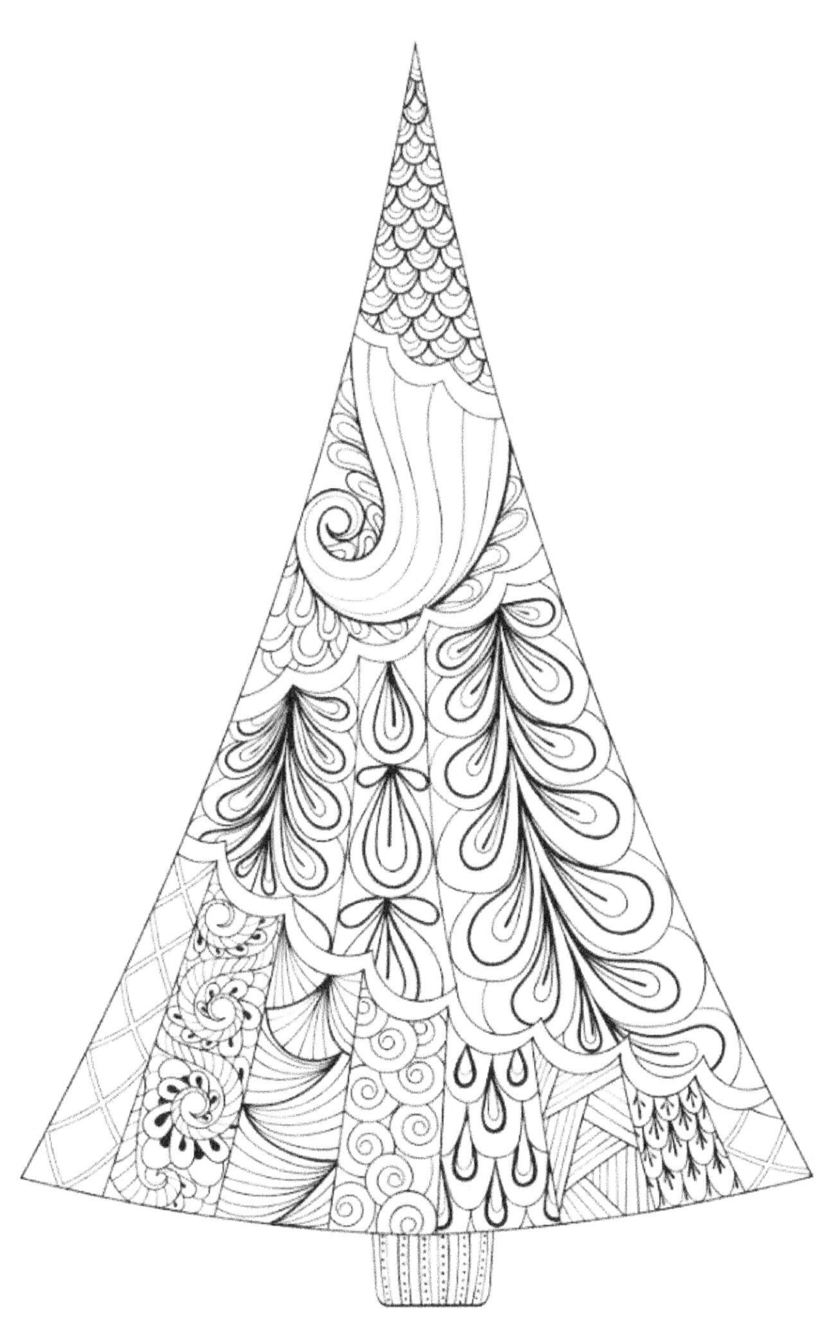

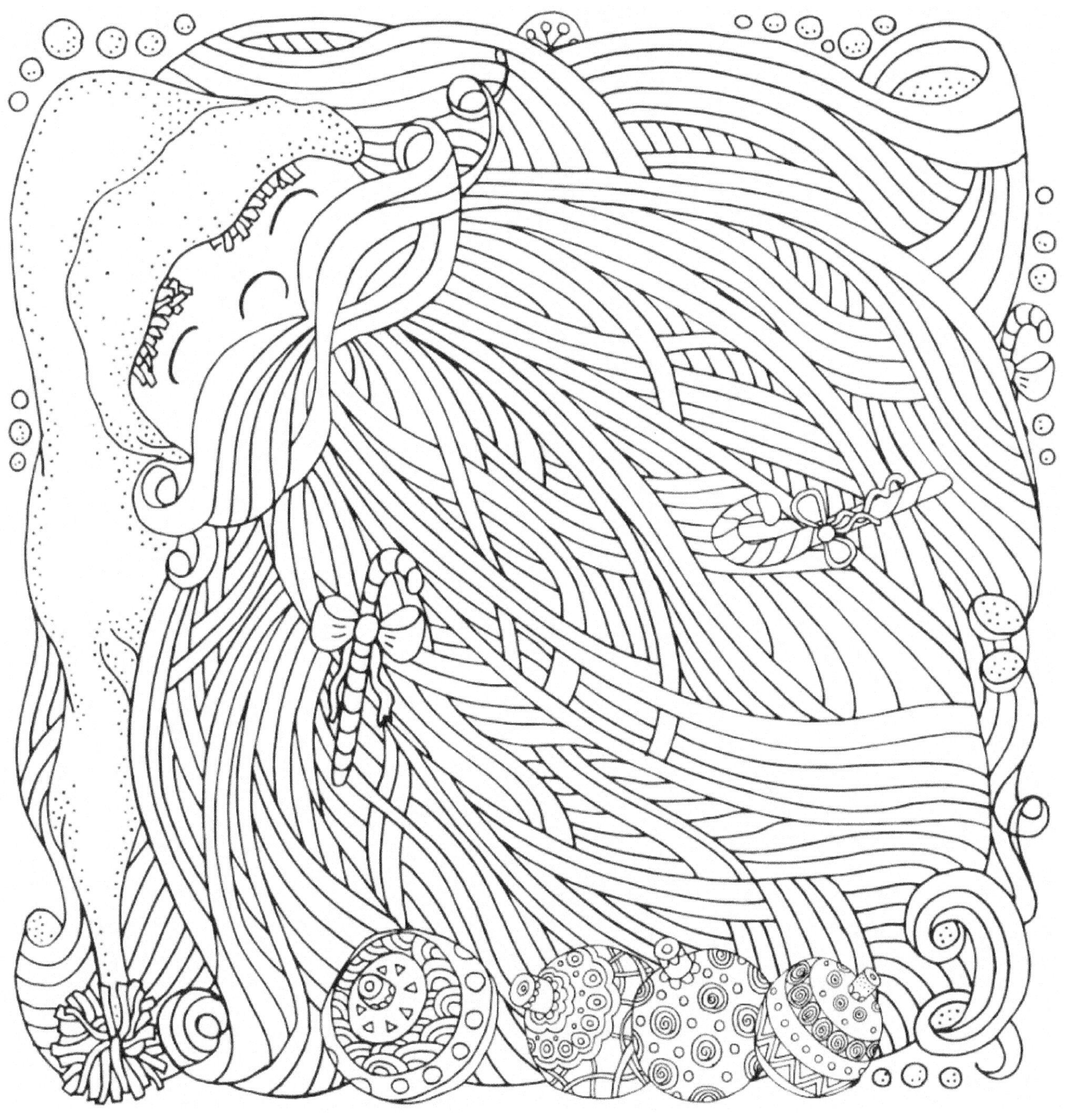

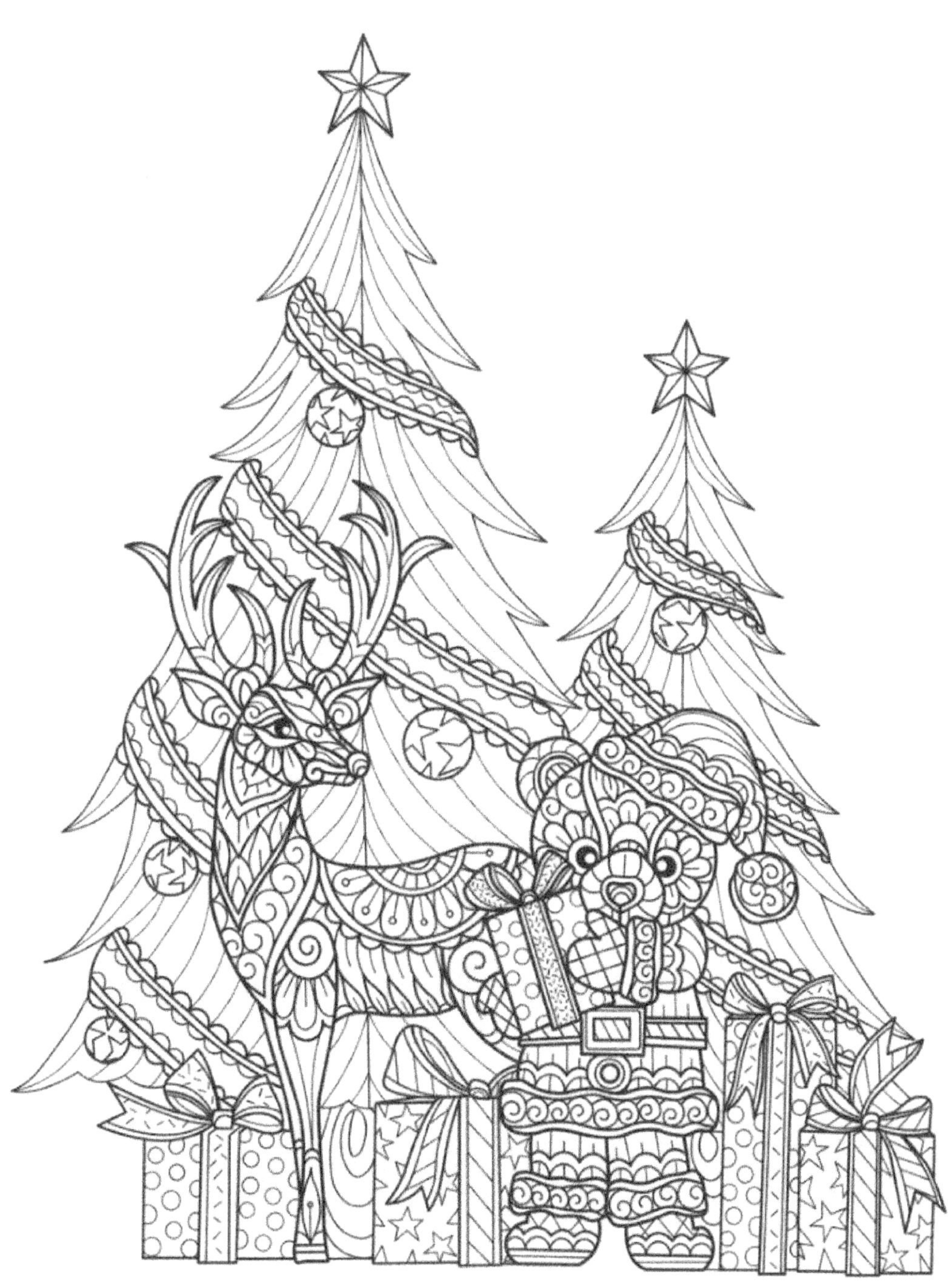

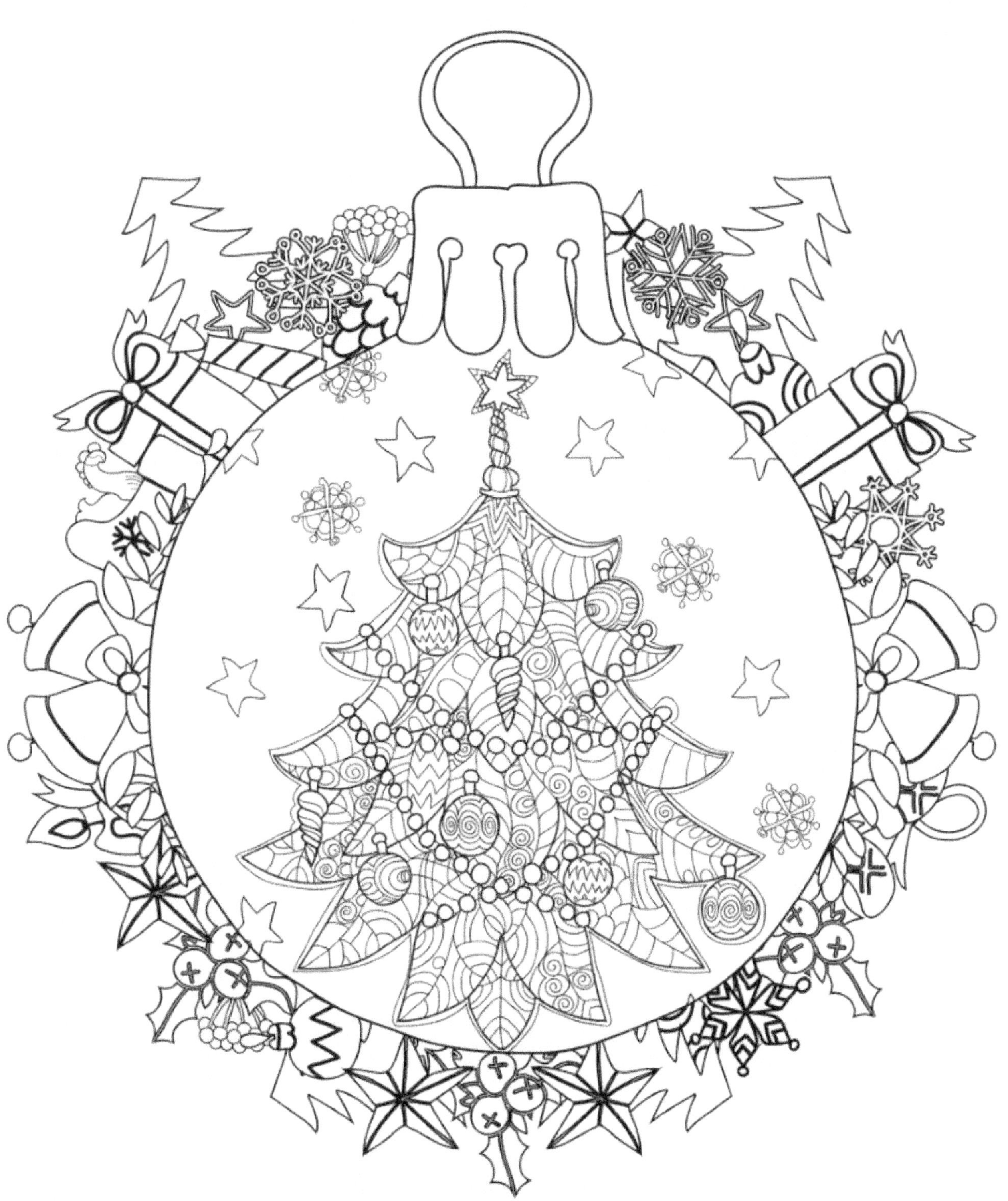

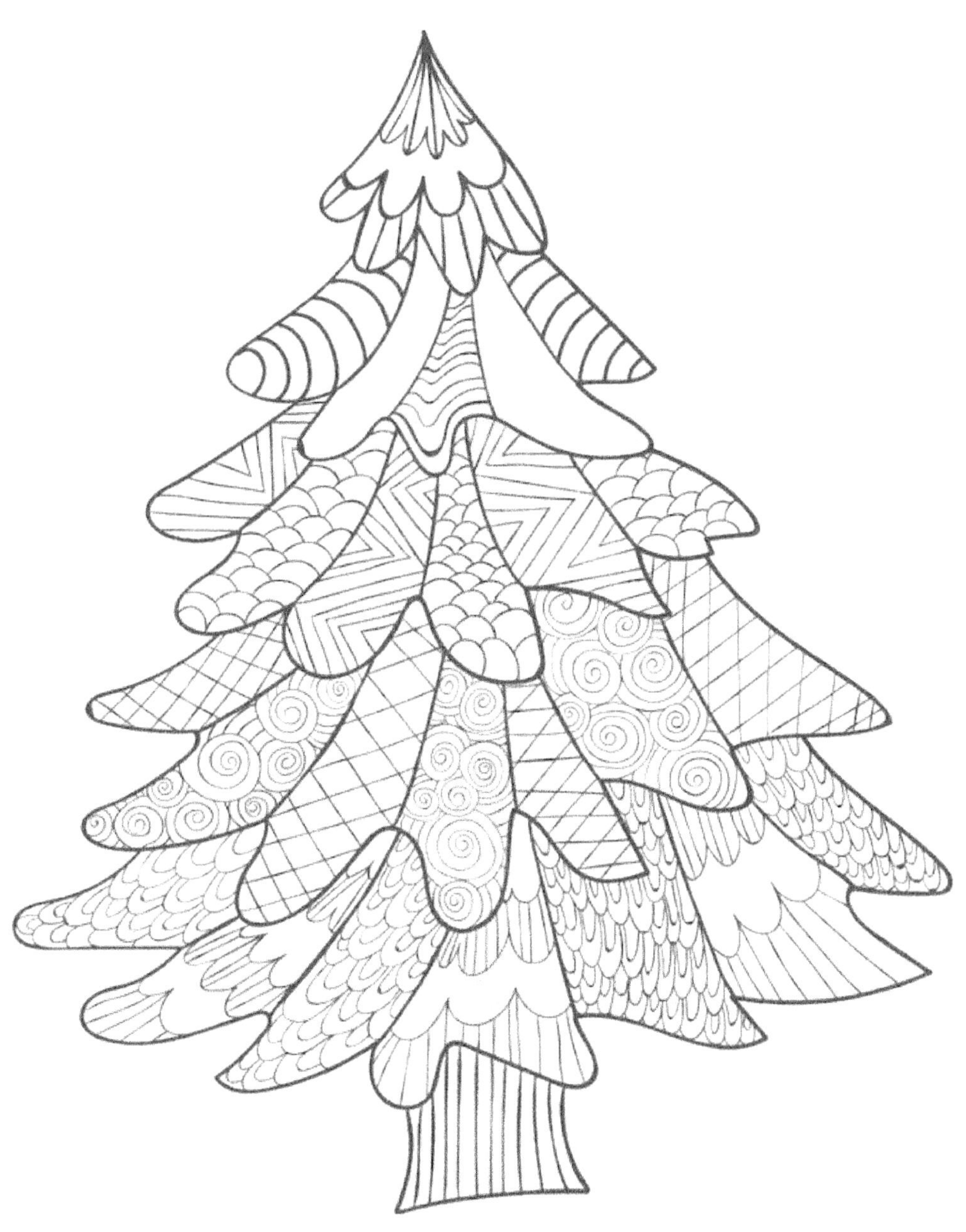

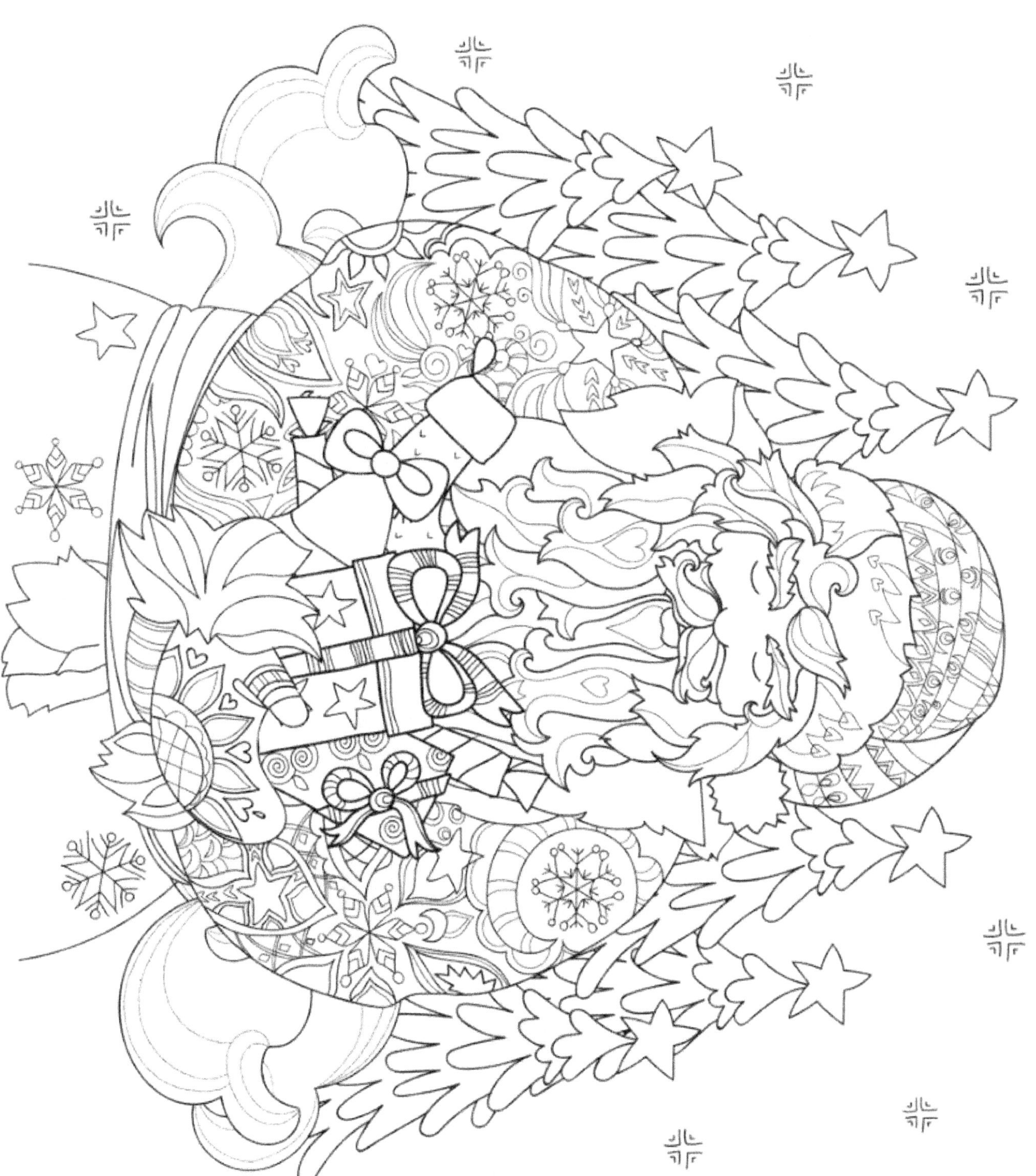

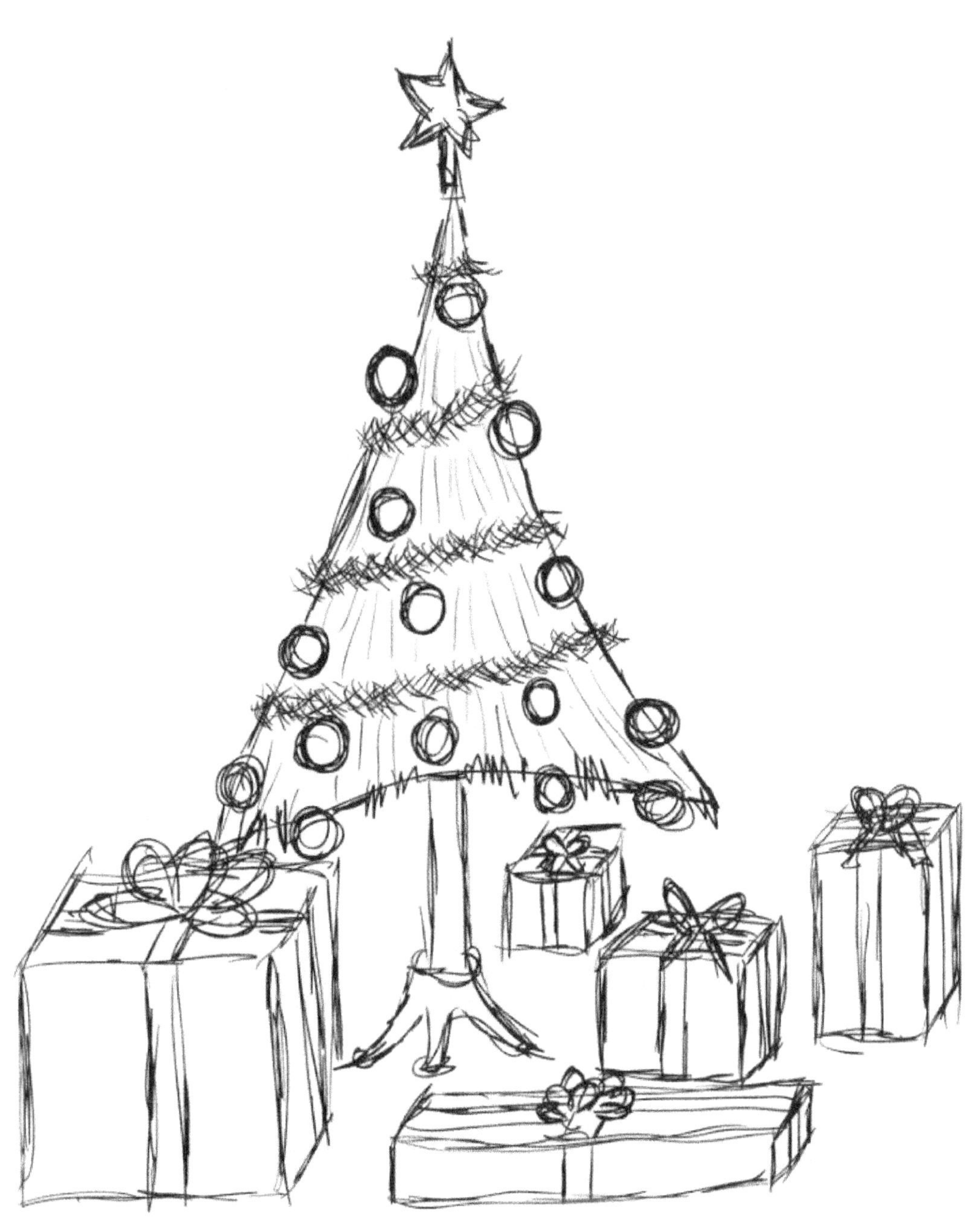

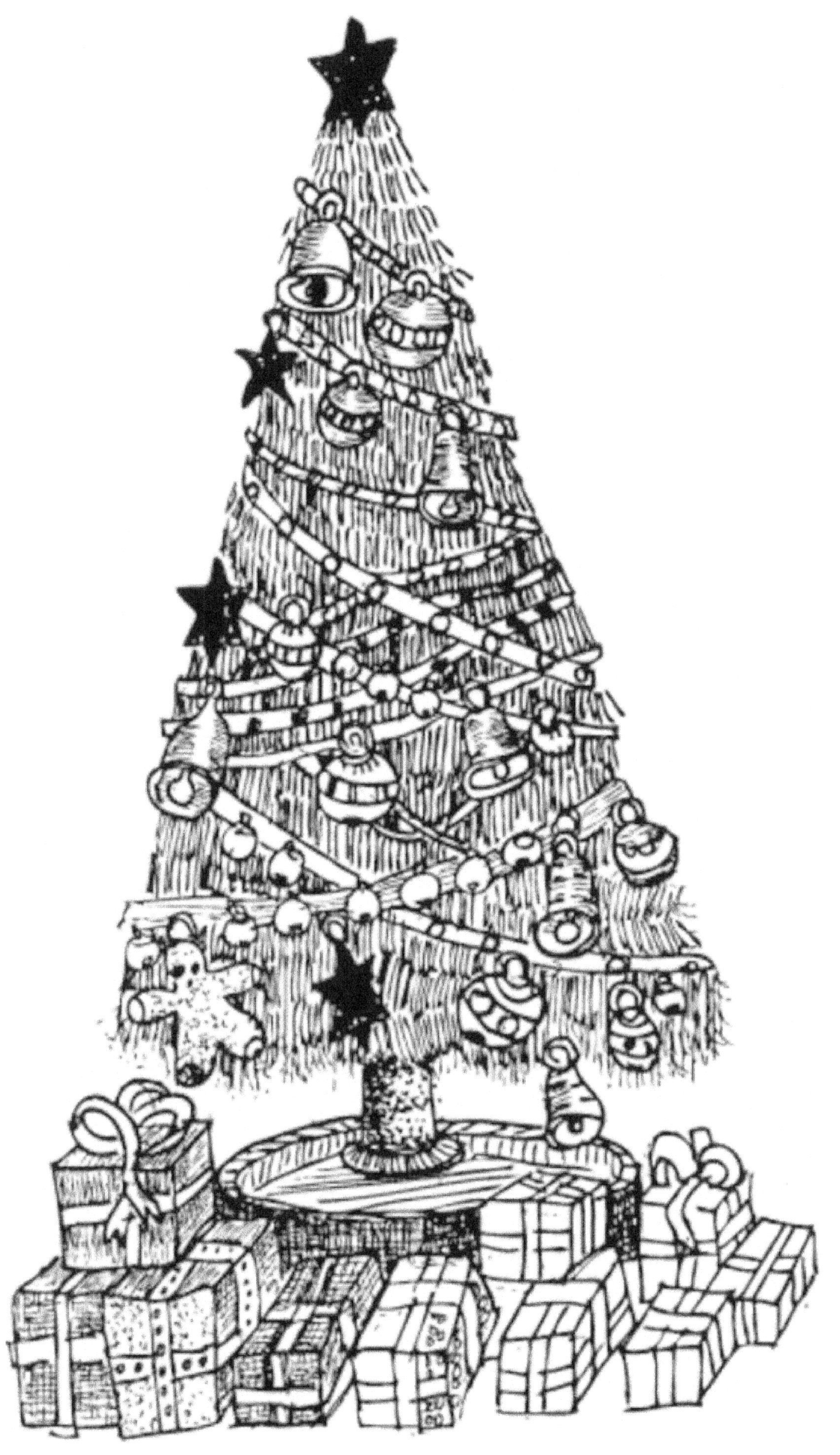

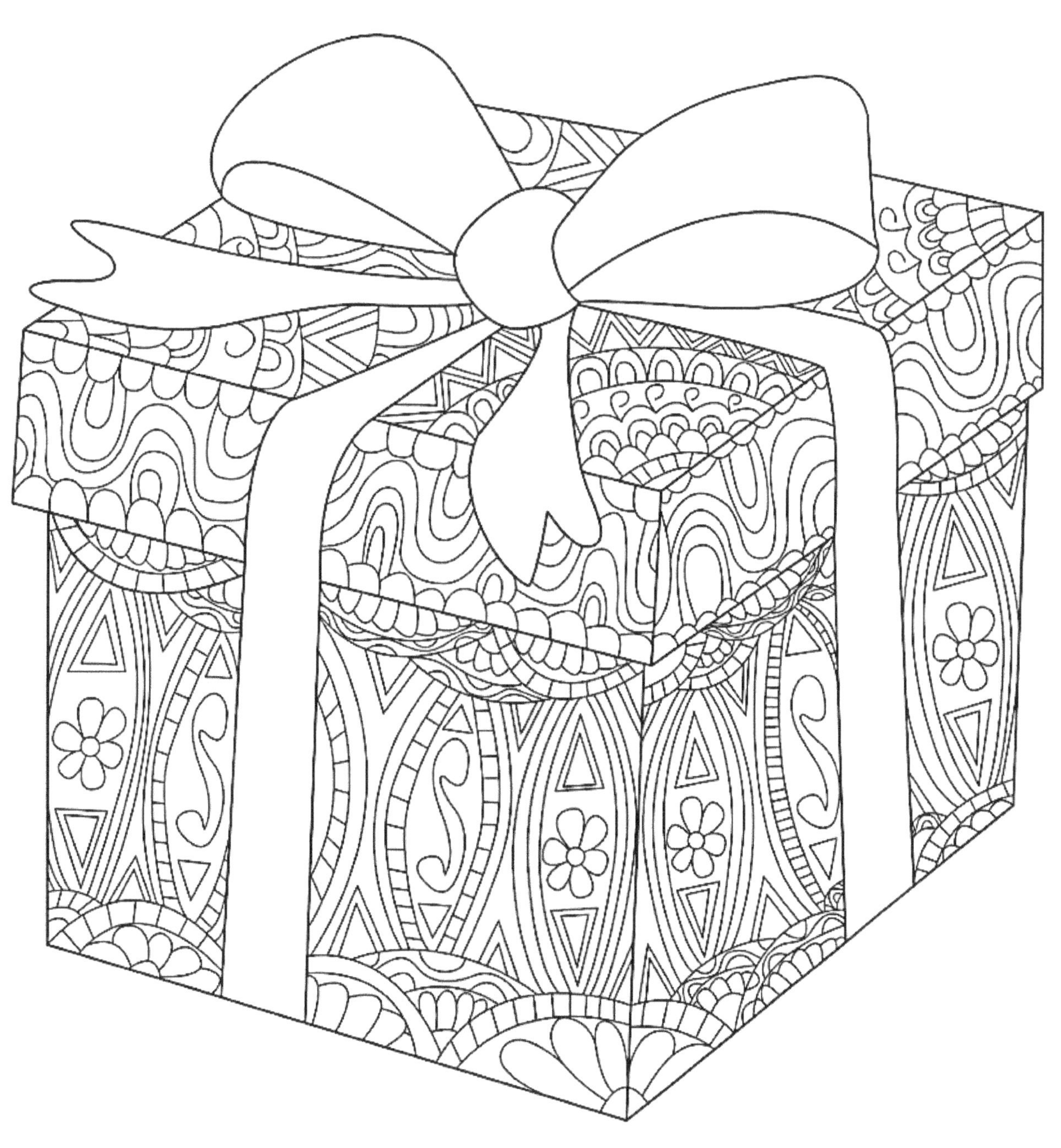

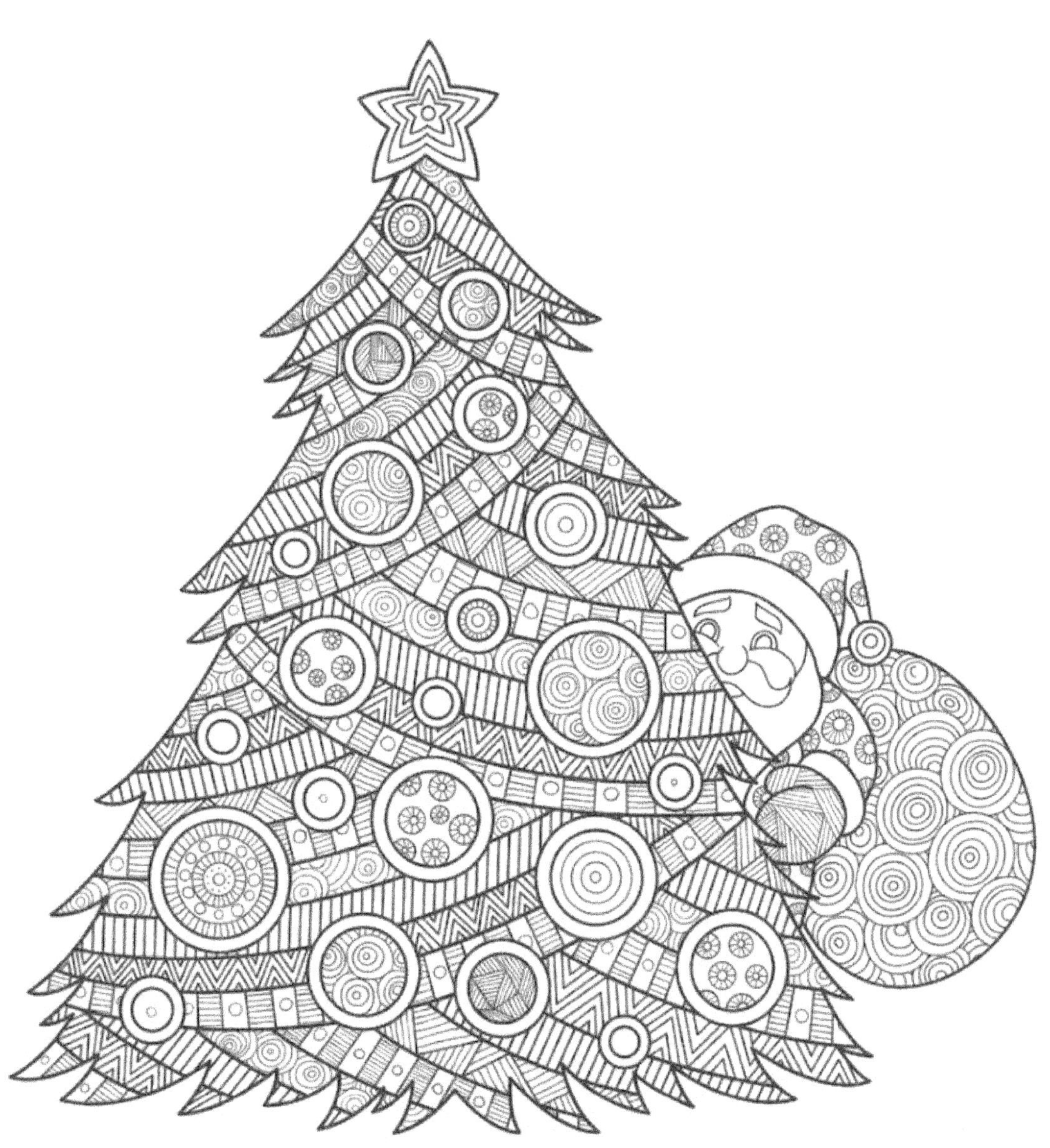

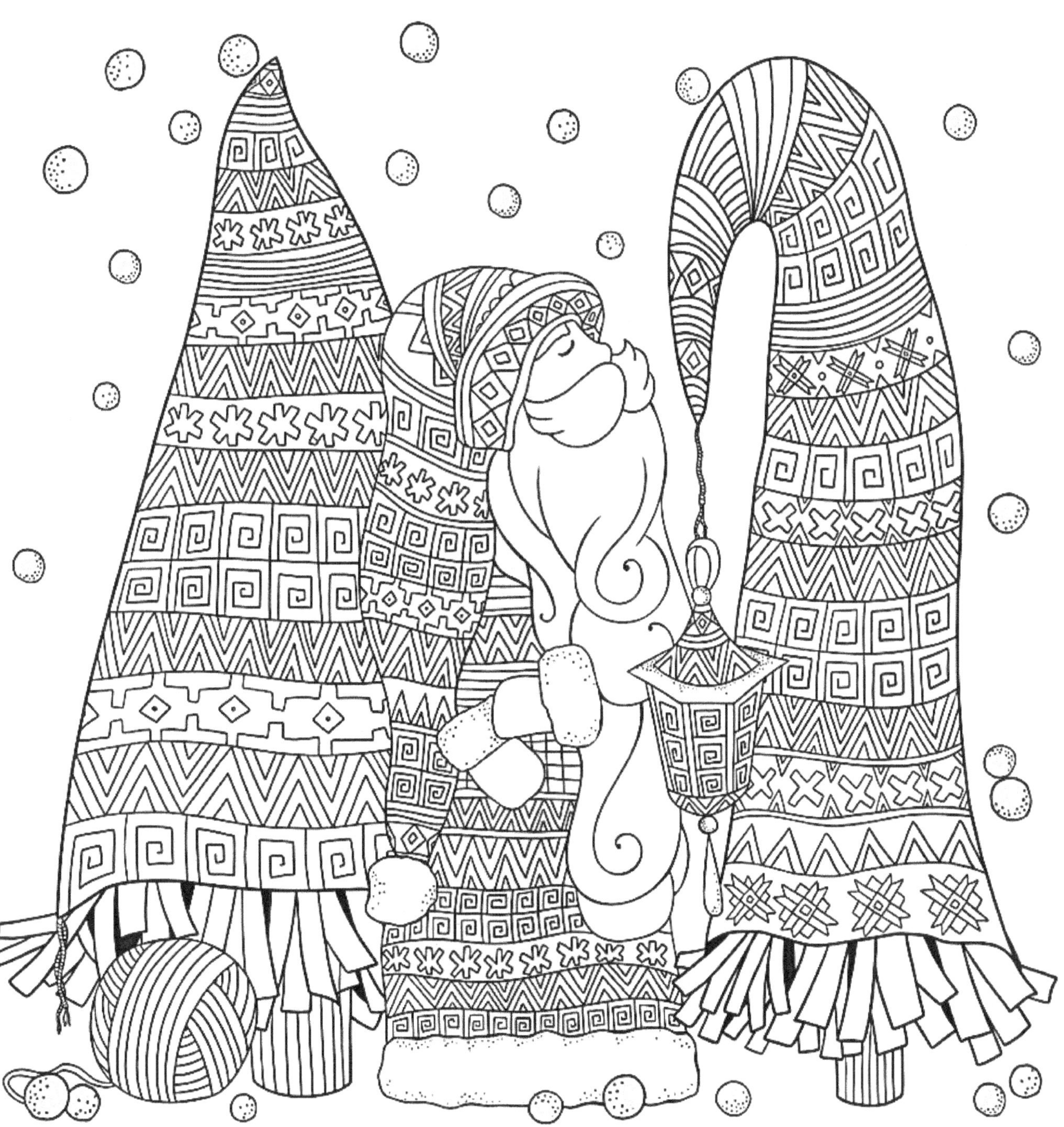

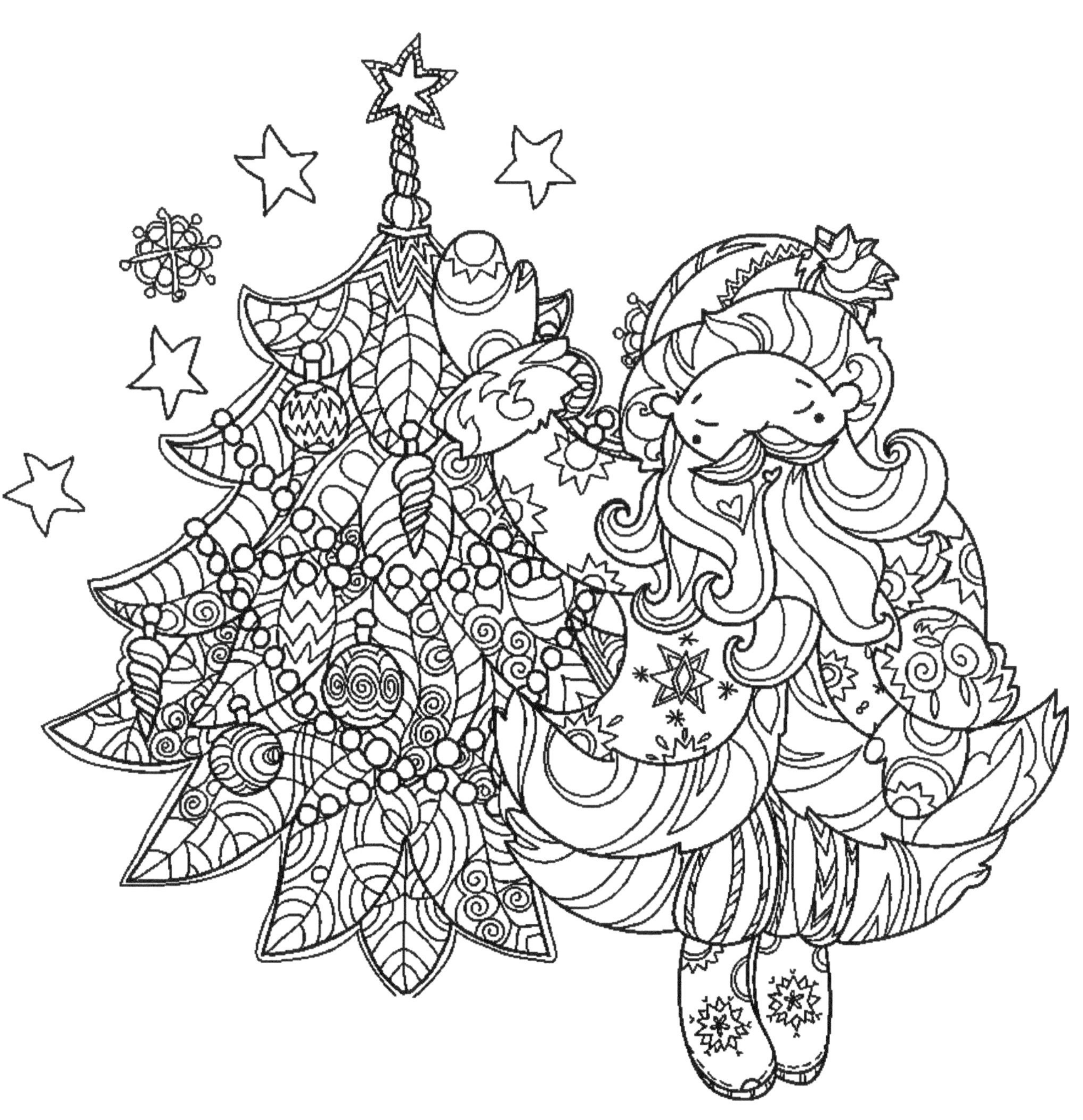

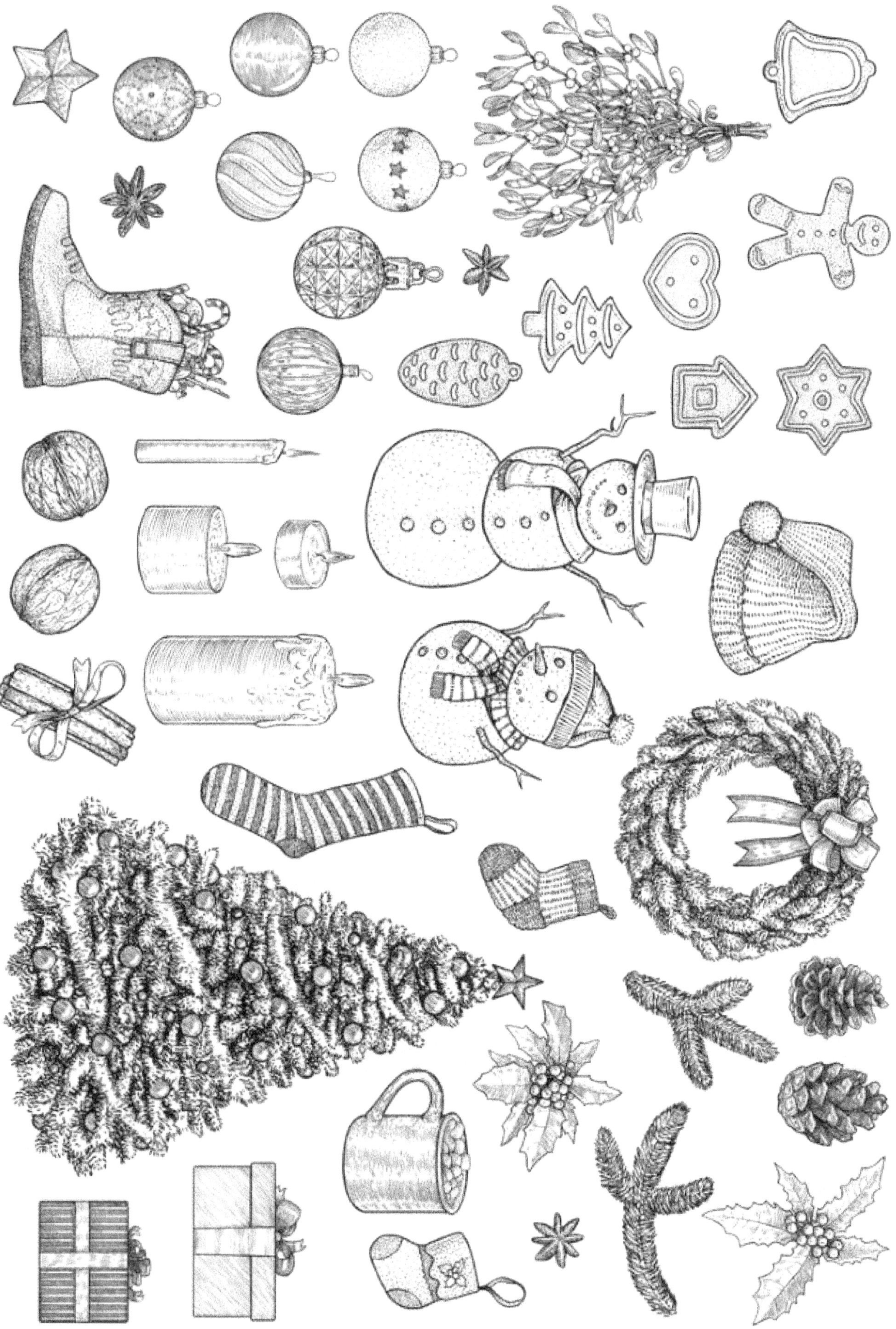

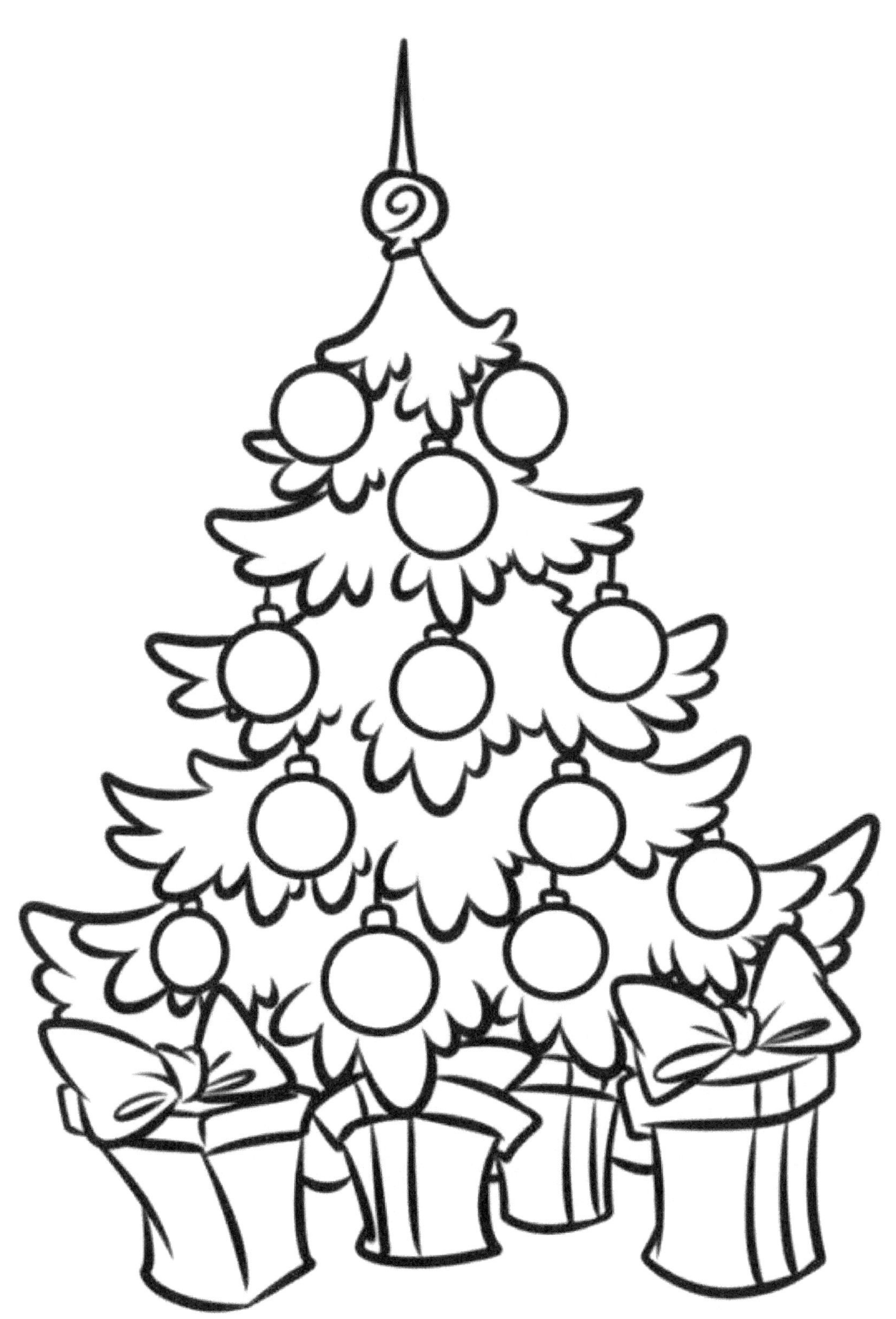

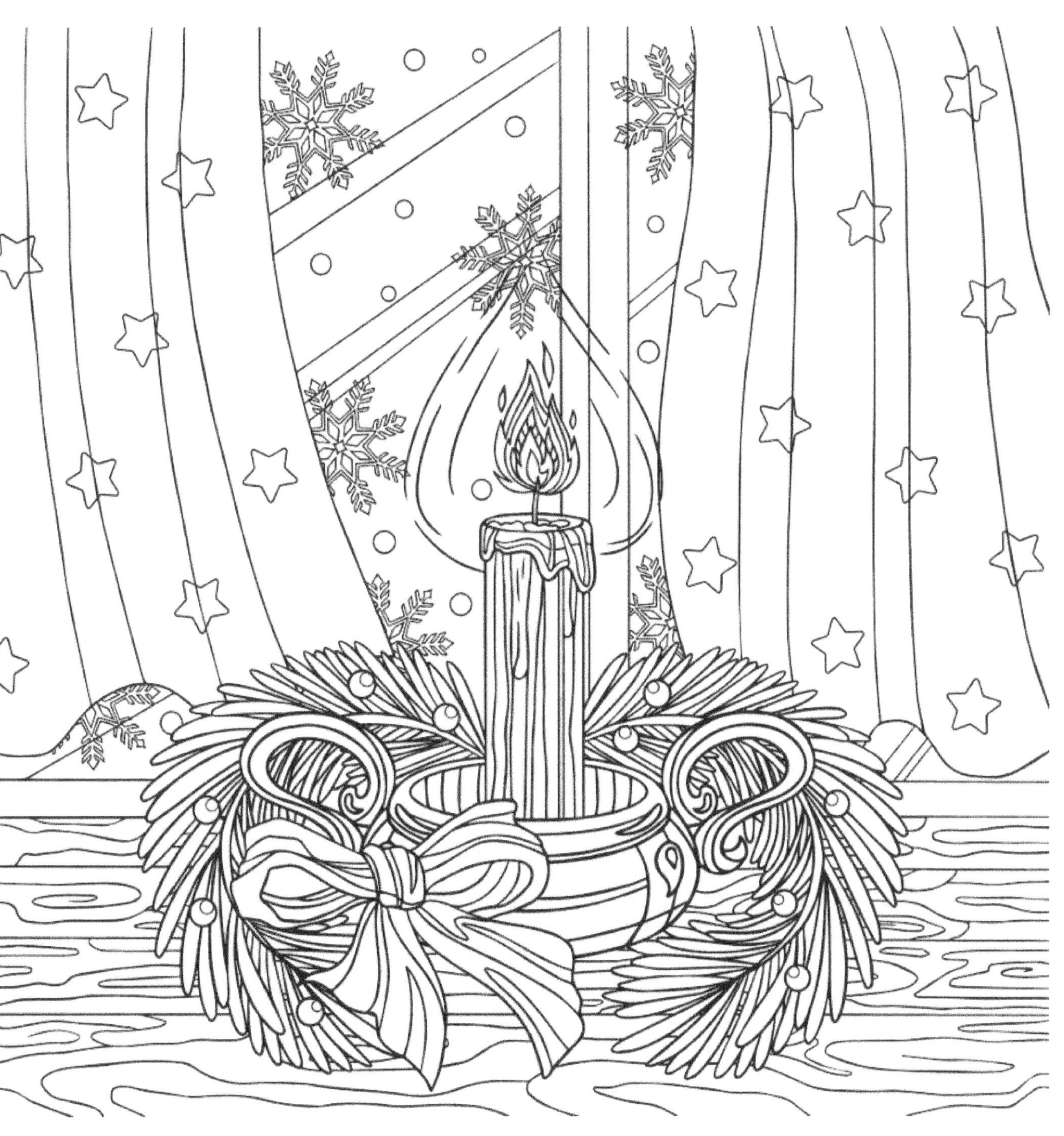

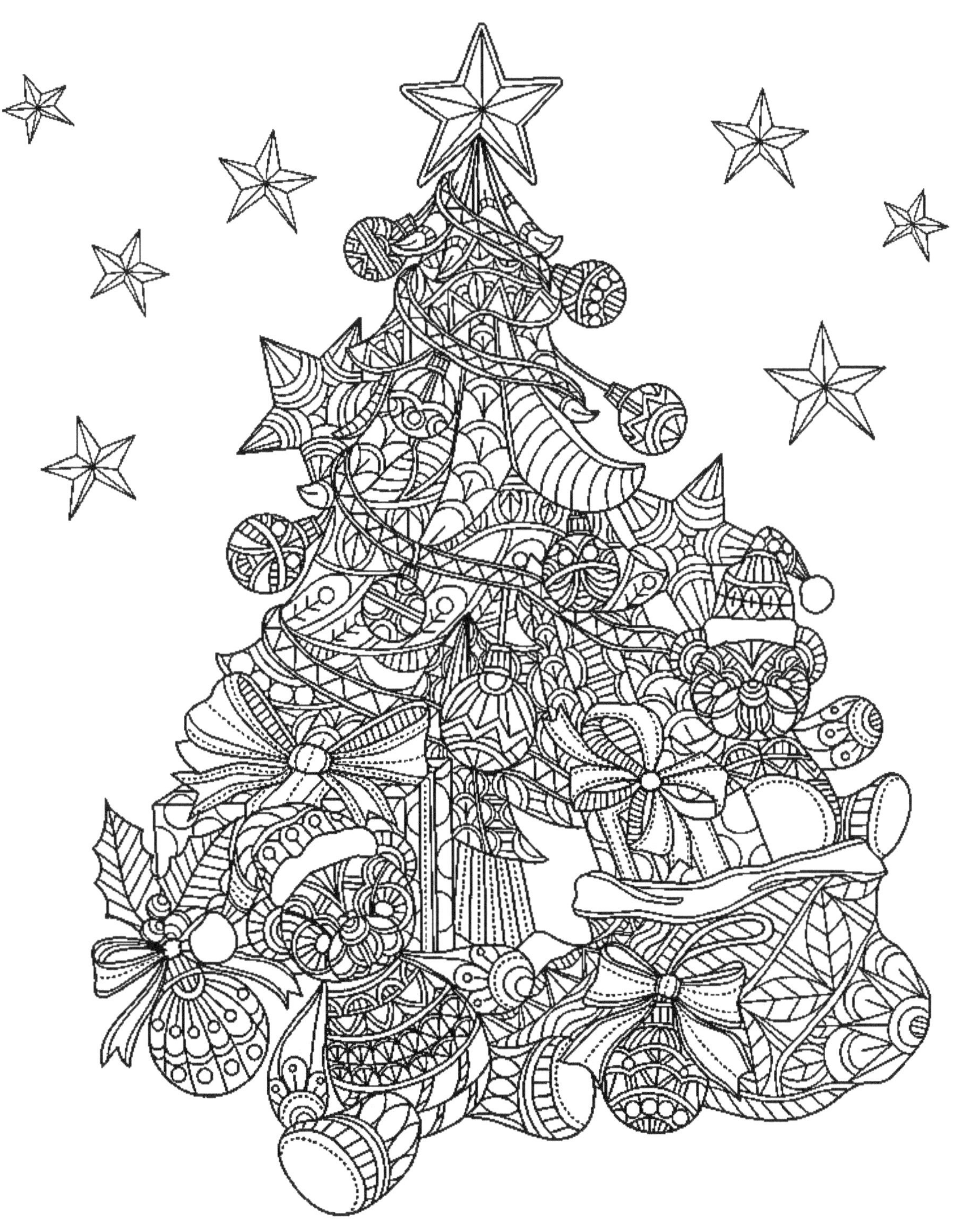

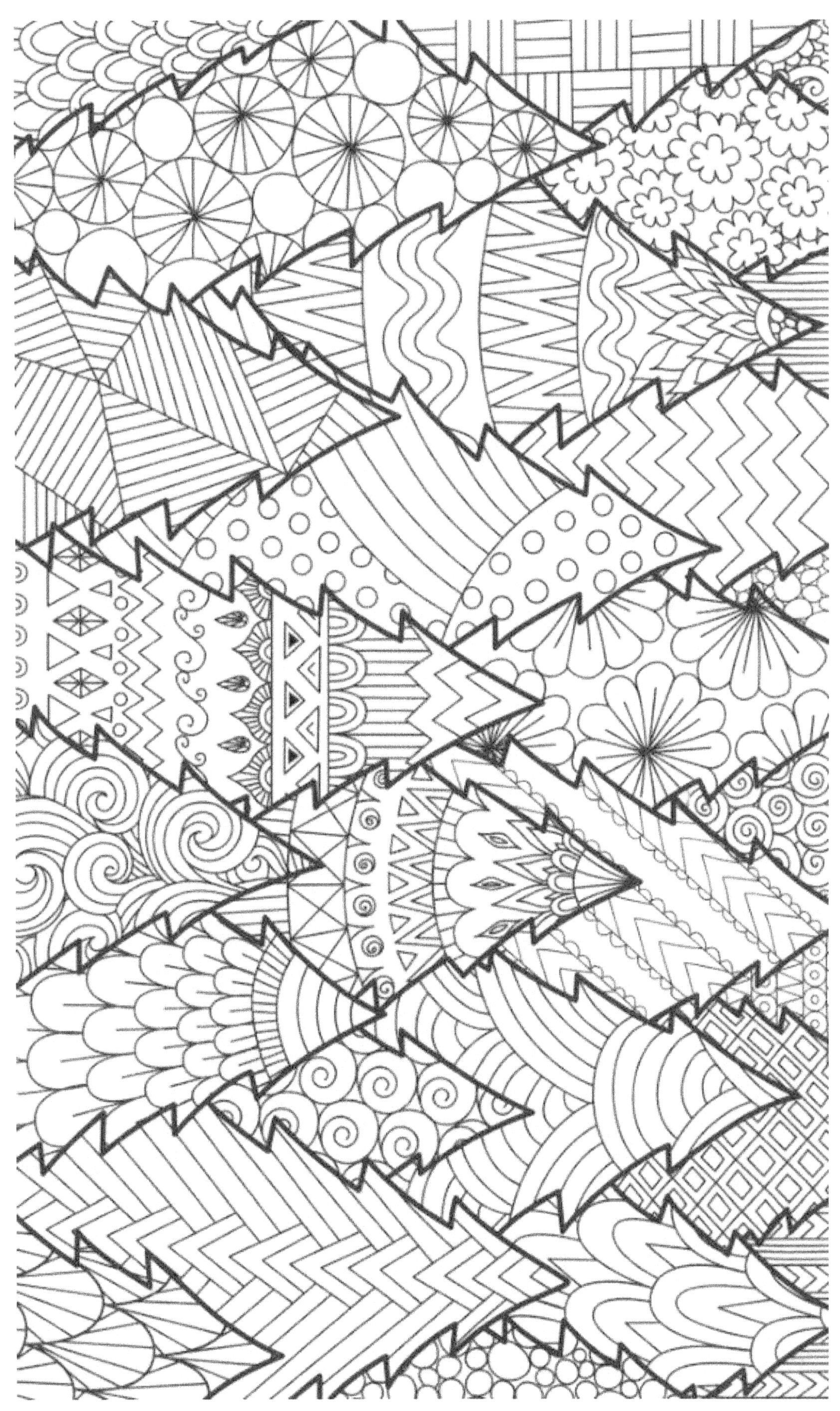

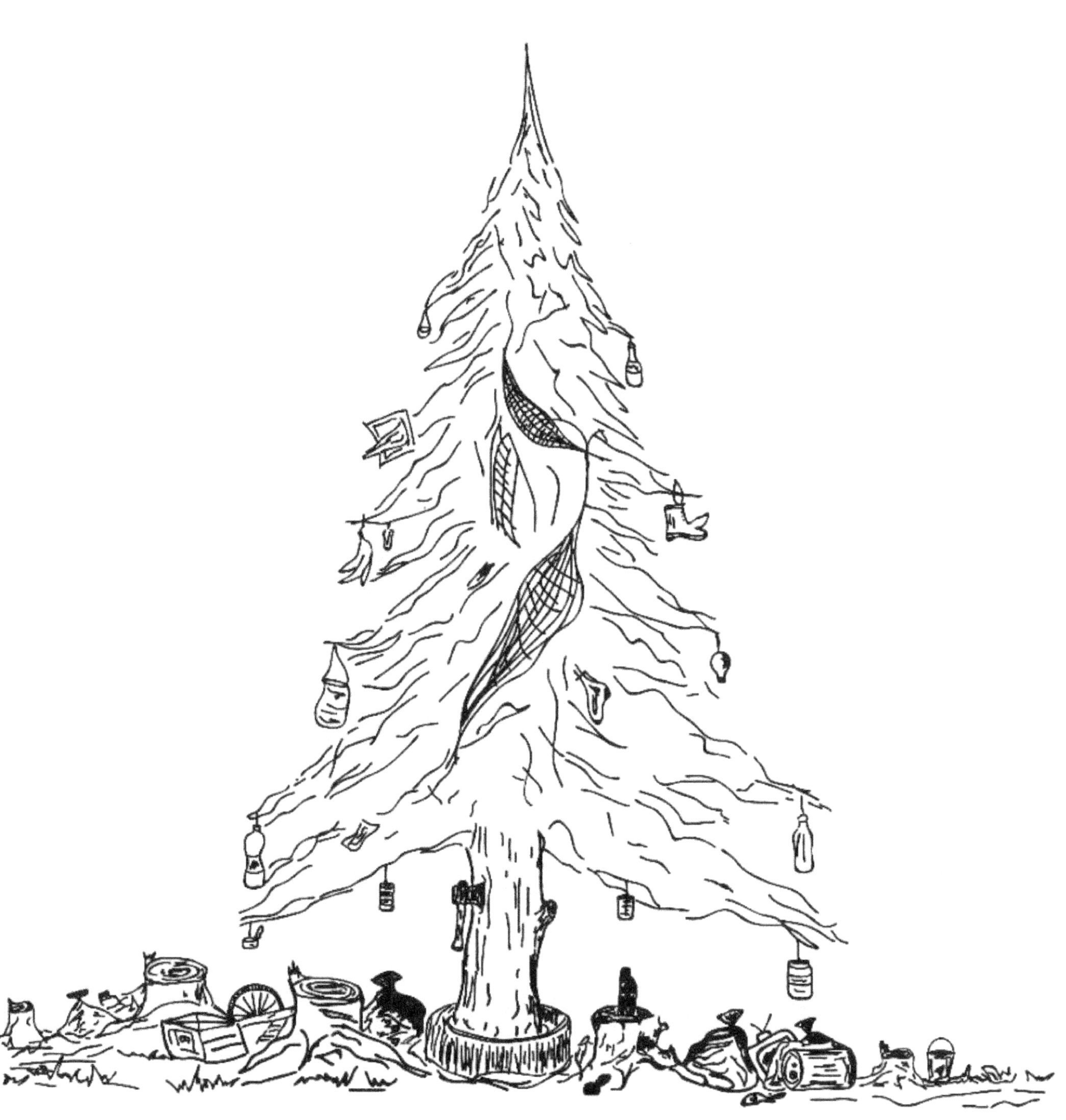

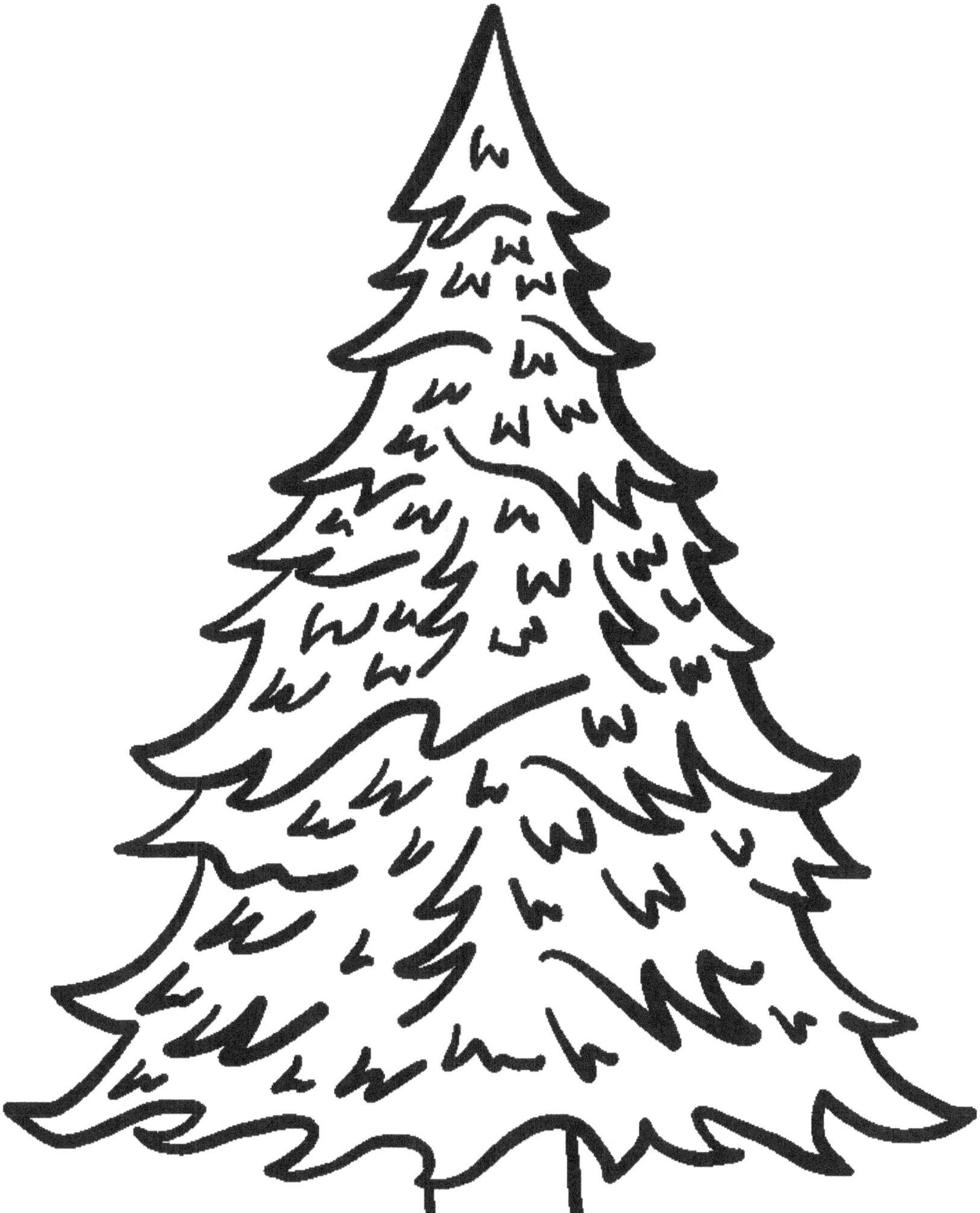

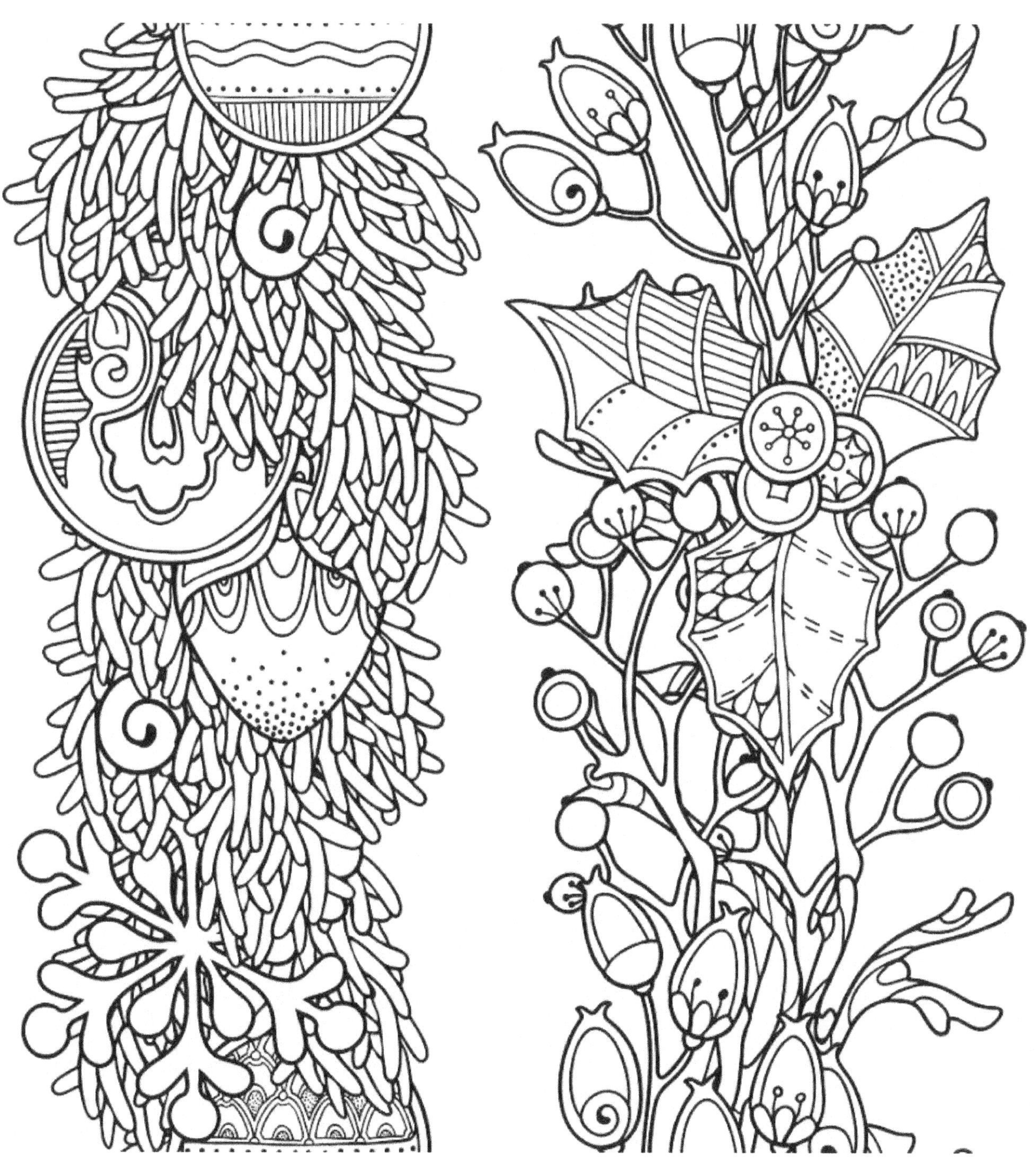

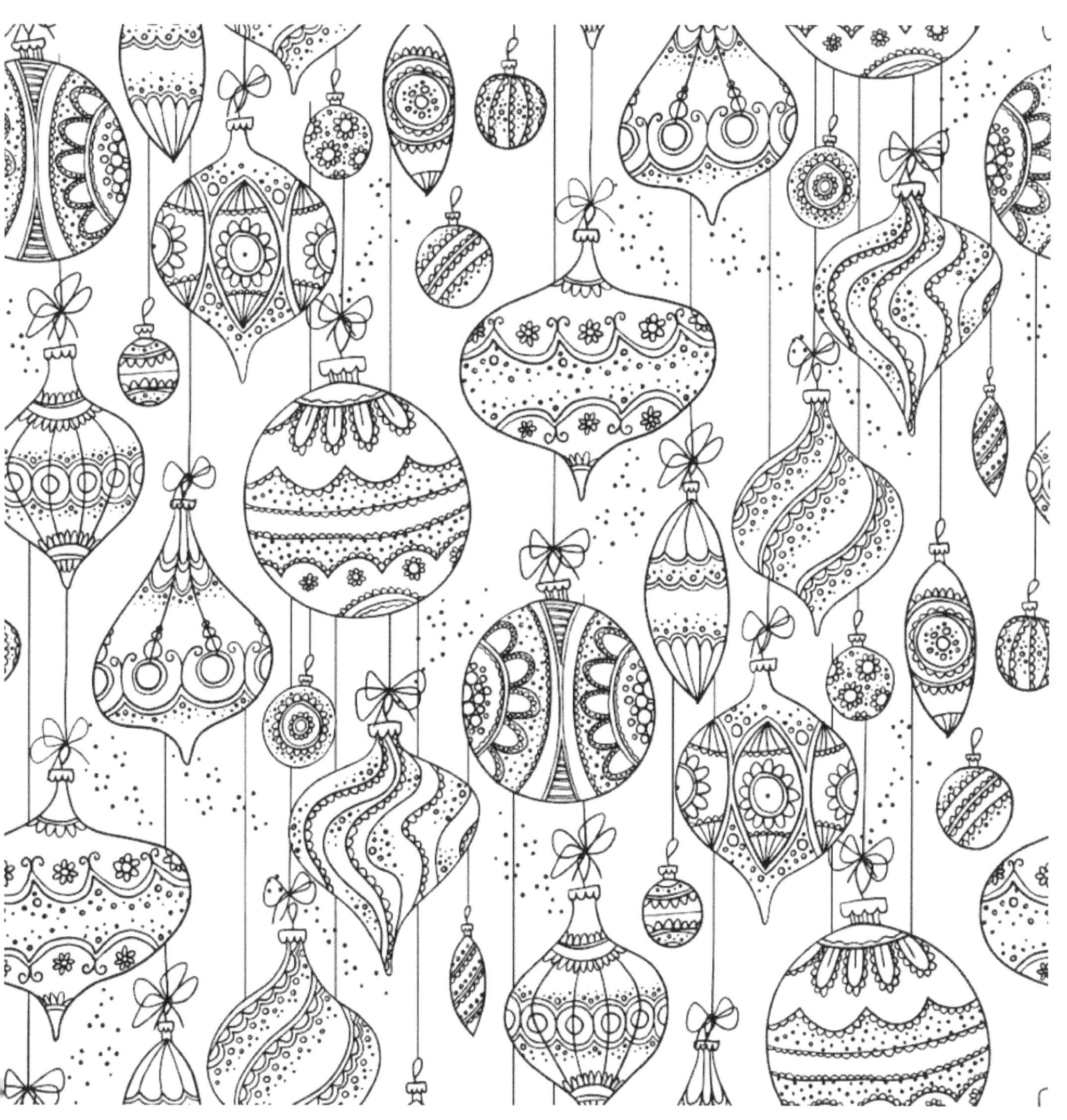

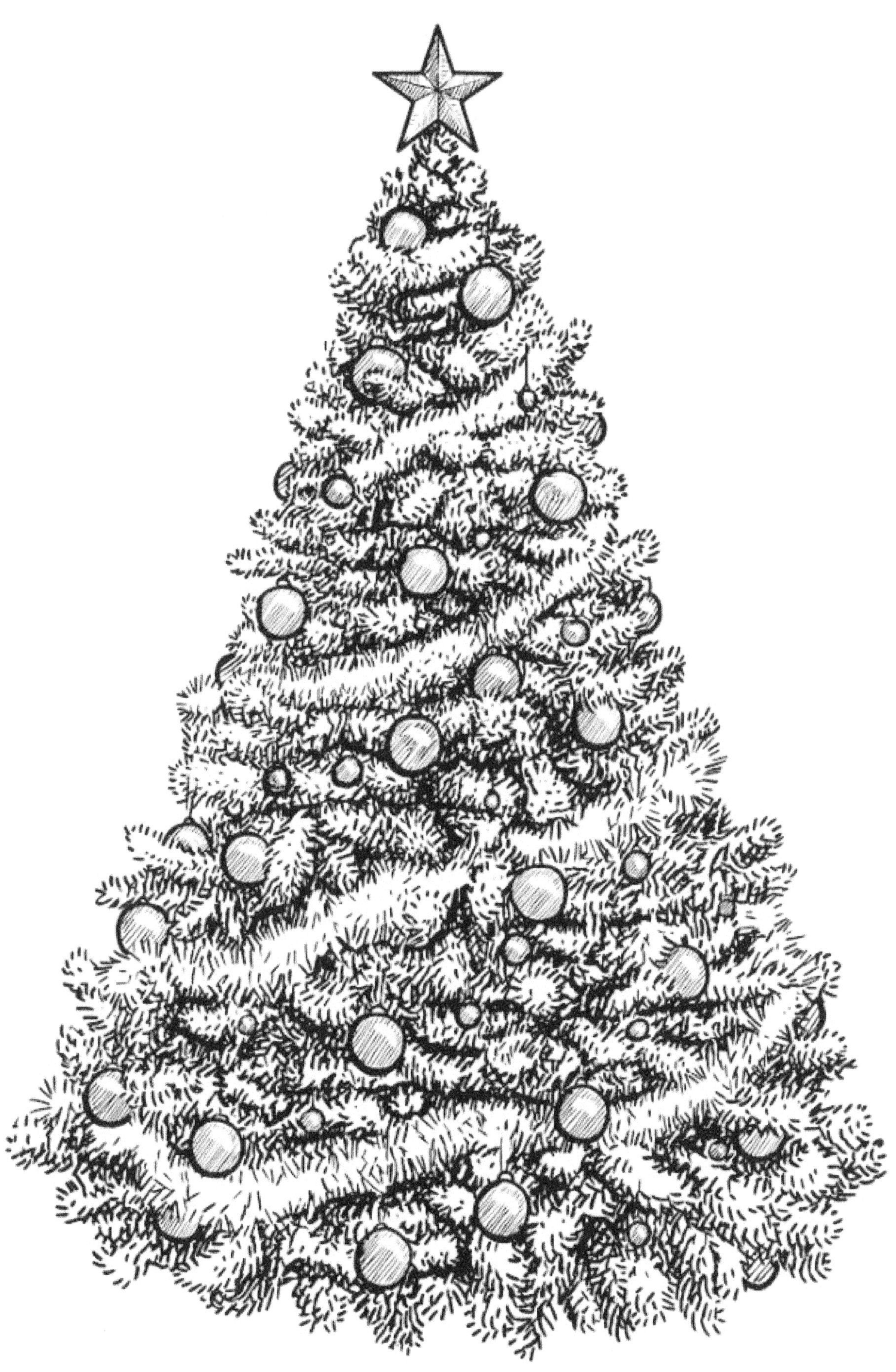

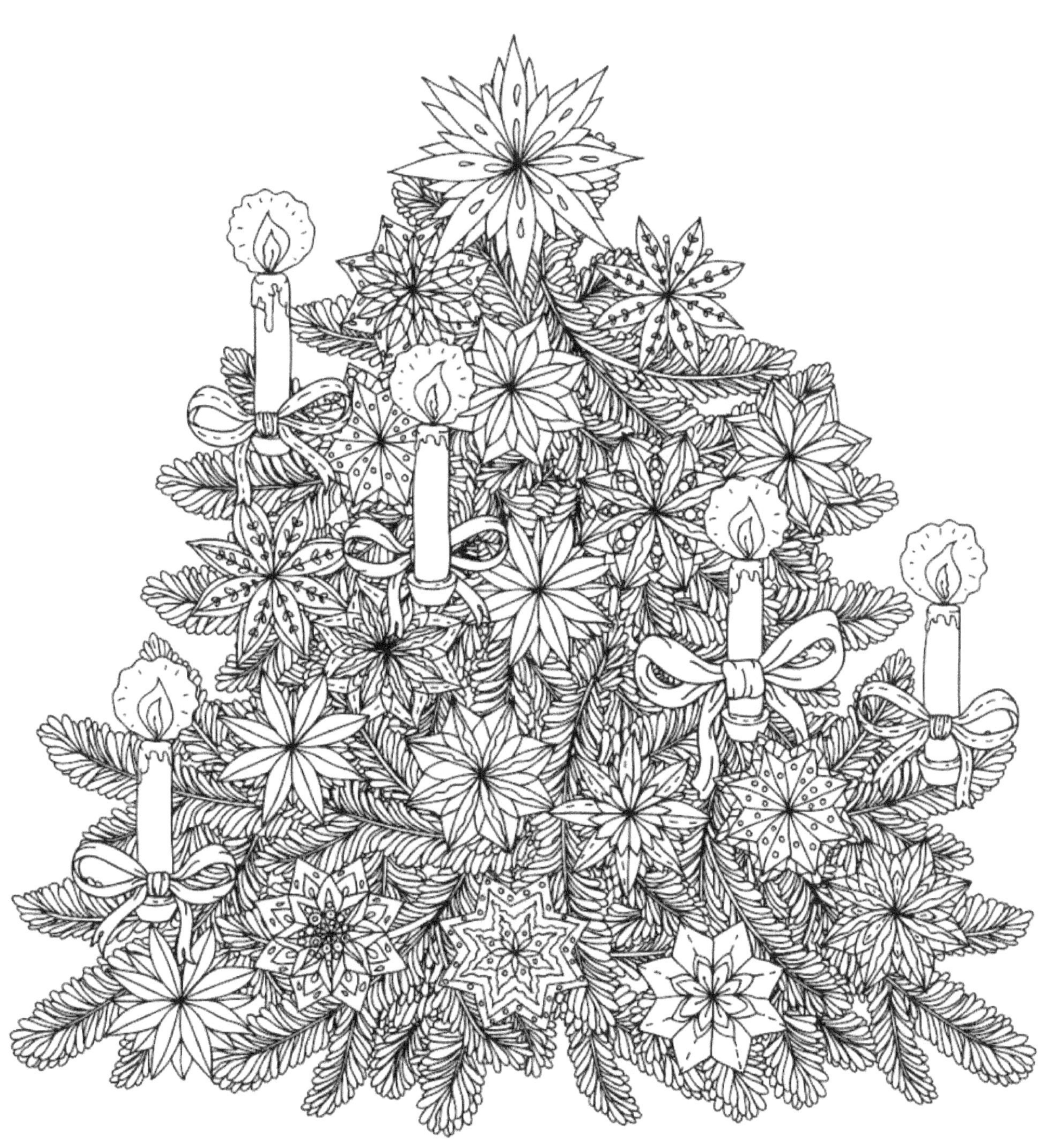

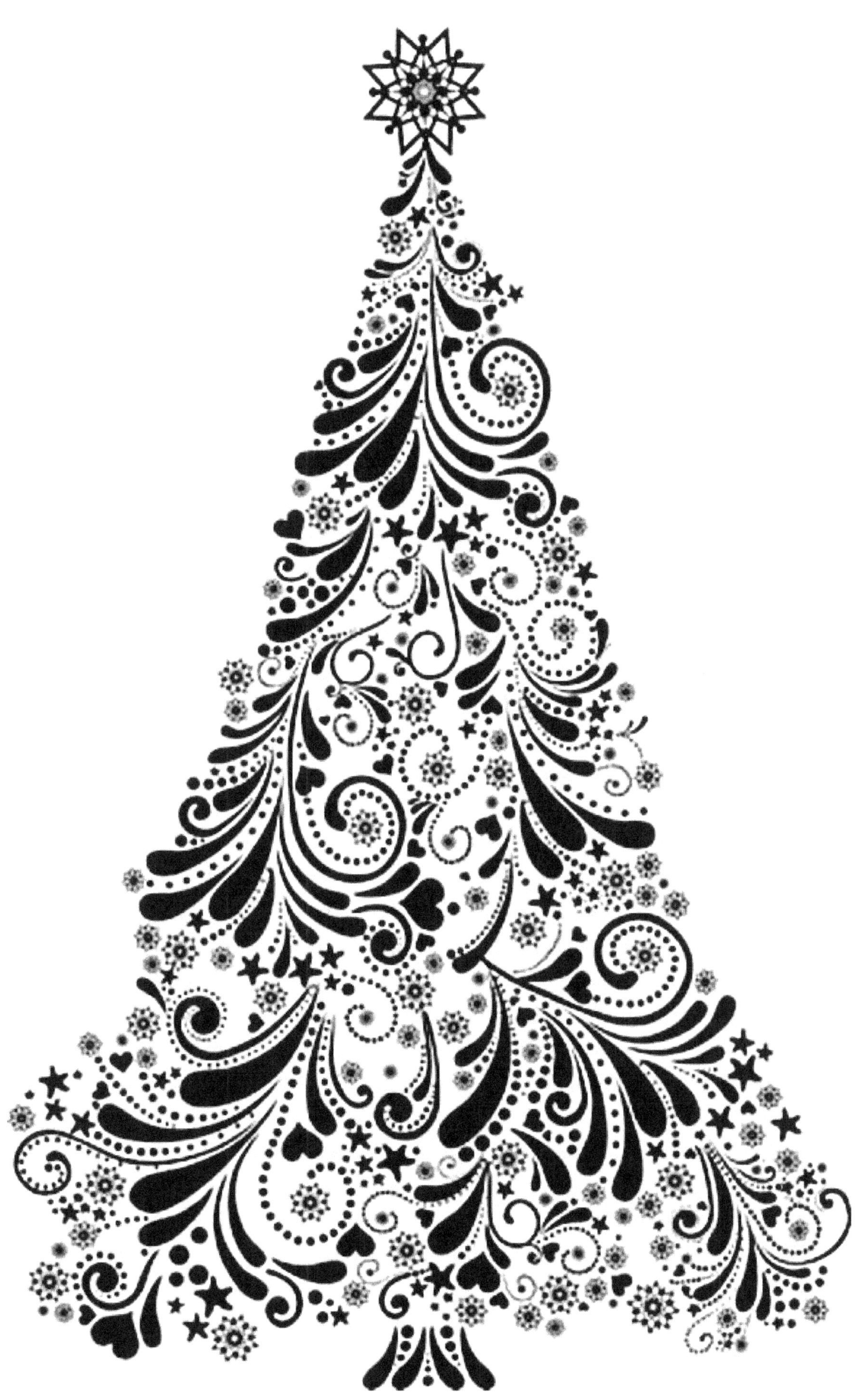

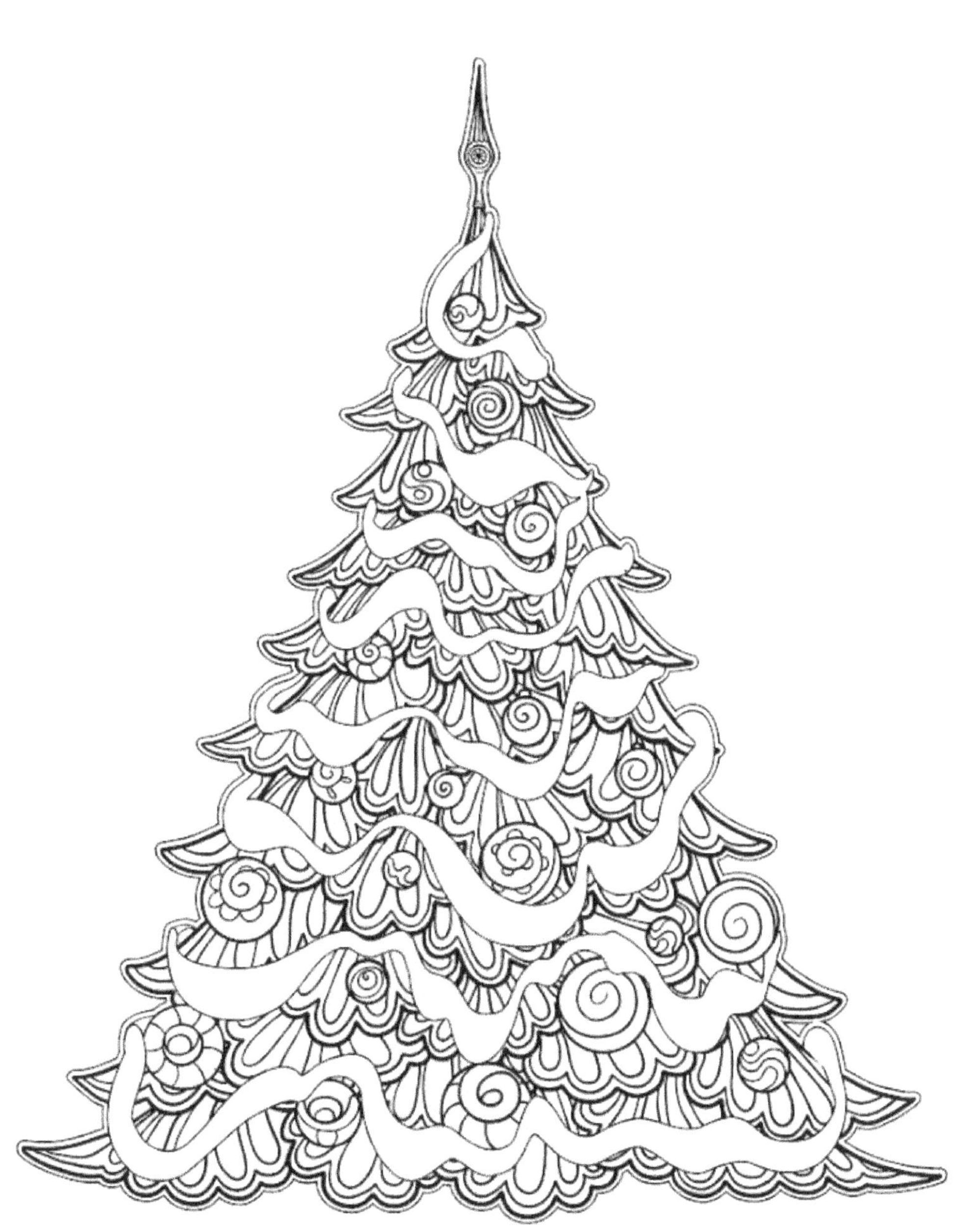

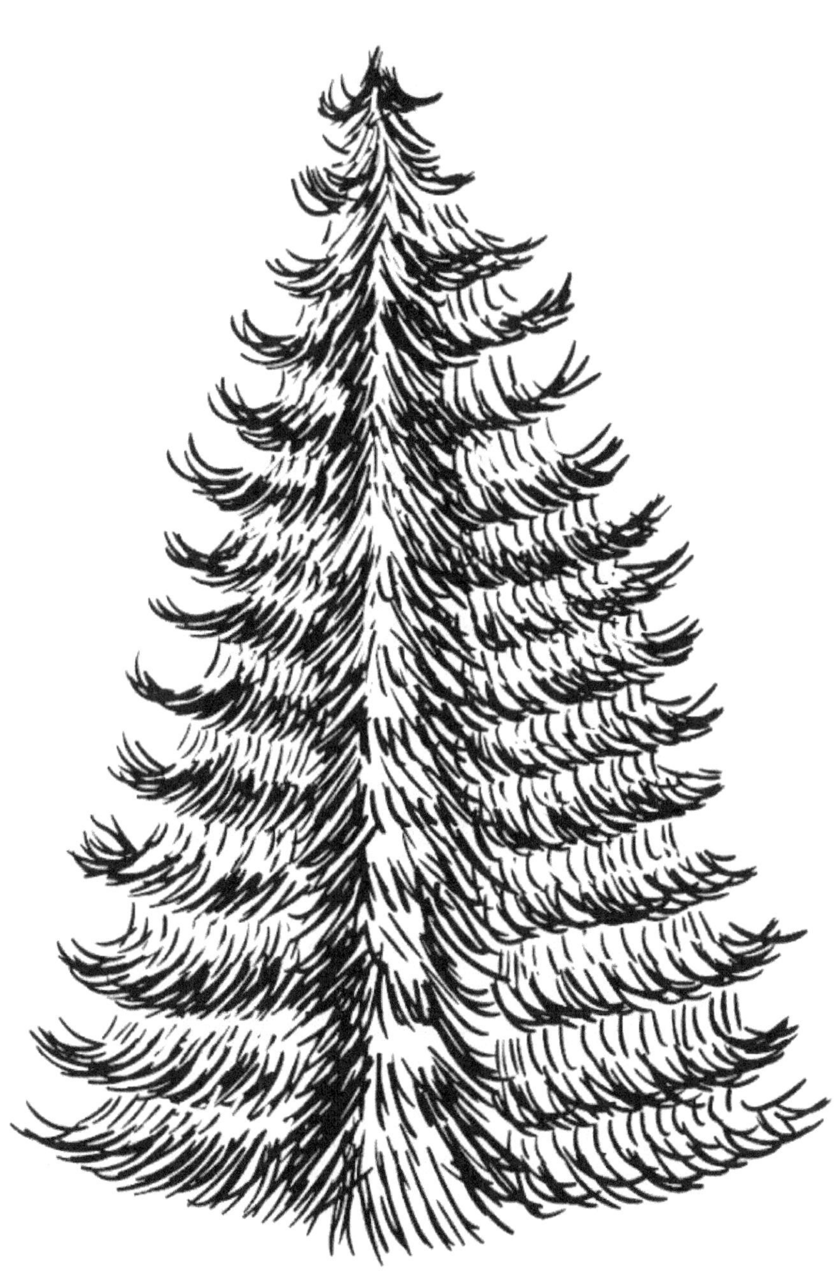

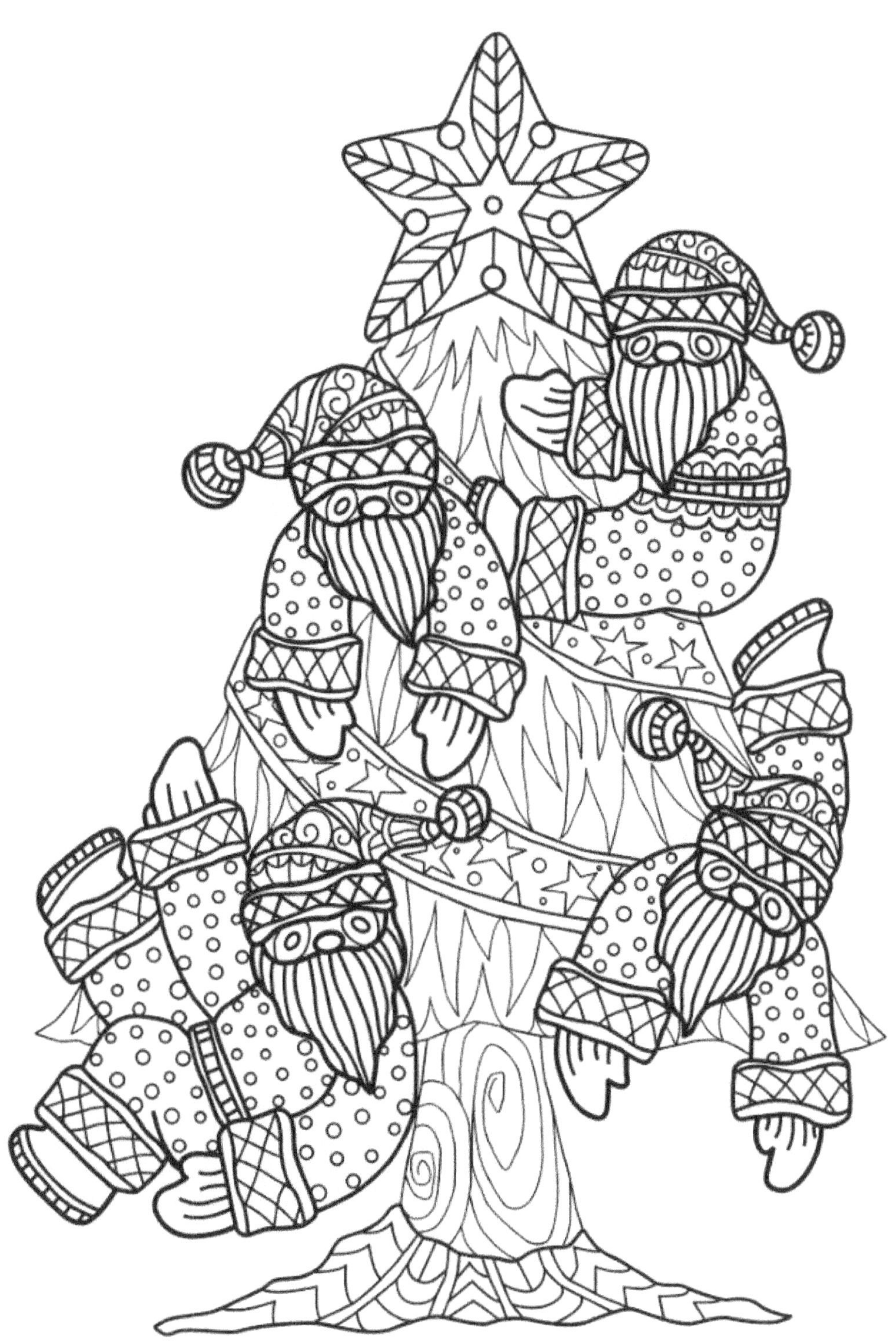

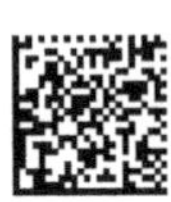